AERIAL FIRE TRUCKS

LARRY SHAPIRO

MBI Publishing Company

Dedication

Tragic events occurred on September 11, 2001, that changed the lives of all Americans and citizens of all countries throughout the world. Terrorist attacks of cowardice in New York City, Washington, D.C., and Pennsylvania claimed the innocent lives of thousands and resulted in many billions of dollars in damage and created far reaching residual effects. Our entire country rallied together showing great strength and solidarity in an effort to overcome and come to grips with what had happened. Specifically related to this book, hundreds of emergency personnel representing police, fire, and EMS agencies in several states responded to these disasters. The horrific loss of innocent civilian life was drastically worsened by the catastrophic building collapses of the World Trade Center towers in Manhattan, which claimed the lives of New York City Police officers, FDNY firefighters, and EMS personnel. Answering the call for help as they did every day, these heroic men and women did not stop to think of their own safety when they advanced into the buildings to rescue the occupants. The greatest loss of life in the history of the FDNY or any fire department will never be forgotten. In the true fashion of the brotherhood in the fire service, firefighters from across the nation, responded to the crisis in New York City by manning firehouses to protect the city, and going to ground zero to offer whatever assistance they could in support of the trapped and deceased rescue personnel and civilians. Without trying to minimize in any way the contributions and unselfish assistance given by non–fire service individuals, one can never forget the images of FDNY personnel emerging from the devastation covered with dust and standing ready to get back into the thick of it.

It is to the commitment and perseverance of those who worked so diligently during and after the events of September 11, 2001, and those who continue to do so every day, that this book is dedicated. In this spirit, they work to preserve the memory of the fallen.

To the memory of the firefighters, EMS personnel, and police officers who perished on September 11, 2001, this book is also dedicated. May they rest in peace.

First published in 2002 by MBI Publishing Company, Galtier Plaza, Suite 200, 380 Jackson Street, St. Paul, MN 55101-3885 USA

MBI Publishing Company books are also available at discounts in bulk quantity for industrial or sales-promotional use. For details write to Special Sales Manager at Motorbooks International Wholesalers & Distributors, Galtier Plaza, Suite 200, 380 Jackson Street, St. Paul, MN 55101-3885 USA.

Library of Congress Cataloging-in-Publication Data Available
ISBN 0-7603-1065-3

On the front cover: A 1995 E-ONE, 95-foot tower ladder is set up as an elevated master stream at an early-morning fire at an abandoned lumberyard.

On the frontispiece: Two model LT-102, LTI tower ladders on HME chassis being used in sector one of the fireground. The Chicago Fire Department assigns sectors to designate each of the four sides of an incident for uniformity of command.

On the title page: In 1981, the New York City Fire Department (FDNY) surprised many in the industry when it ventured outside of the Aerialscope product line for the first time and ordered two midship, 100-plus tower ladders from Sutphen. TL119 was stationed in Brooklyn with a very busy company.

On the back cover, Bottom: A 1995 100-foot Seagrave Patriot Series tractor-drawn aerial from Ventura, California.

Top 2: The FDNY utilizes nothing but Seagrave aerials for its fleet of straight ladders. Ladder 6, stationed in Chinatown, was assigned this new ladder in 1984. The fully enclosed, four-door, H-Series cab allows room for the entire truck company crew.

Edited by Kris Palmer
Designed by Stephanie Michaud

Printed in China

Table of Contents

Acknowledgments

I have been photographing fires and fire trucks since before I was 15 years old, and have always hoped for an avenue to share my images with others. What better way to achieve this goal than through the opportunity to write books? This is my third book about the fire service, and regardless of the knowledge that I think I have about this subject, I certainly don't consider myself an expert. This is why I have enlisted the expertise, experience, and knowledge of others who have dedicated their lives to various aspects of the fire service. Each person listed below has made a significant contribution to the research and compilation of the information included in the following chapters. My sincerest gratitude is extended to every one of them, in addition to those people that I have inadvertently omitted through any oversight.

In fairness to all, the names are listed alphabetically.

Jeff Aiken, E-ONE; Bill Burch, Schwing America, Inc.; Tom Goyer, E-ONE; Helen Haase, formerly with Pierce Manufacturing; Dan Herb, The Sutphen Corporation; Peter Hoherchak, KME Fire Apparatus; Ben Hoppe, formerly with FWD Seagrave; Jay Johnson, E-ONE; Sonya Kelly, E-ONE; Ken Lenz, HME; Deputy Chief Neil T. Lipski, Milwaukee Fire Department; Bill McCombs, E-ONE; Art Moore, formerly with Snorkel Fire Apparatus and Pitman Manufacturing; Doug Ogilvie, formerly with Pierce Manufacturing; Steve Redick; Harvey Roth, FWD Seagrave; Kirsten Skyba, Oshkosh Truck Corporation; Bryan Smeal, Smeal Fire Apparatus; Tim Smits, Pierce Manufacturing; Tom Sutphen, The Sutphen Corporation; and Bob Vanstone.

Special thanks also go to certain individuals who worked to create the history that is included in this book and therefore were in a unique position to help assure accuracy in recording the historical facts related to several companies. The persons mentioned above are listed with the companies they are or were associated with. To mention the names of others with their current positions though does not fairly acknowledge the contributions that each person is responsible for. Listed below are names with their current positions, as well as details of their previous service to the fire apparatus industry.

Jack Bailey Jr., KME Fire Apparatus, formerly with Ladder Towers, Inc. and Grumman Emergency Products; R. J. "Bob" Barraclough, formerly with Class 1, Span Instruments, Emergency One, Hale Pumps, and National Foam Systems; Bill Bruns, UPF Fabrication, formerly with Ladder Towers, Inc. and Grumman Emergency Products; Dennis Chamberlain, Spartan Motors, formerly with Ladder Towers, Inc. and Grove Manufacturing; Eli Ebersol, American LaFrance, formerly with Ladder Towers, Inc.; Earl Everhart, VTEC, formerly with Mack, Maxim, Hendrickson Mobile Equipment, and FMC Fire Apparatus Division; Ralph Fiorillo, formerly with Firewolf and Grumman International Inc.; Richard J. Gergel, formerly with Ward '79 Limited, Pemfab Trucks, Mack, and Ward LaFrance; Rob Haldeman, American LaFrance, formerly with Ladder Towers, Inc.; Gary Handwerk, Hale Products, formerly with American Fire Pump, Quality Manufacturing, Carmar, Hammerly, Custom Products, and Hahn Motors; Jim Hebe, formerly with American LaFrance and Ward LaFrance; Randy Hummer, American LaFrance, formerly with Ladder Towers, Inc.; Rob Kreikemeier, founder of R.K. Aerials, formerly with Smeal Fire Apparatus; Jim Johnson, formerly with FWD-Seagrave and Pierce Manufacturing; Gene Lough, KME Fire Apparatus, formerly with Grumman Emergency Products; Tony Mastrobattista, American LaFrance, formerly with Ladder Towers, Inc.; Al Morganelli, formerly with Emergency One and FMC Fire Apparatus Division; Tom Nist, formerly with Boardman and Readi-Tower Corporation, Reading Techmatic, Ward LaFrance, and American LaFrance; I. Dean Riley, Grove Worldwide, formerly with Ladder Towers, Inc. and Grove Manufacturing; Paul Stevenson, Hendrickson Suspensions, formerly with E-ONE; Glenn R. Vanderspiegel, formerly with Aerialscope, Inc. and Baker Engineering; Saralyn Wagers, American LaFrance, formerly with Snorkel Fire Apparatus; "Sparkey" Webster, Aerialscope, Inc., formerly with Peter Pirsch and Sons, and Ward LaFrance; Dave Wilhide, formerly with General Safety, Aerial Innovations, Ladder Towers, Inc., and Grove Manufacturing; Reid Wissler, American LaFrance Aerials and Aerial Innovations, formerly with Ladder Towers, Inc.; Kevin Zimmerman, American LaFrance Aerials and founder of Aerial Innovations, formerly with Ladder Towers, Inc.; Mahlon Zimmerman, American LaFrance and Aerial Innovations, Inc., formerly with Ladder Towers, Inc.

In each book I've written, I saved a special section to thank someone who was and still is very important to me, and without whom I would have been unable to complete the monumental task required of assembling this project. It is my wife, Dorothy, who keeps me going, provides endless encouragement, is always supportive, and musters the energy and perseverance to read and reread the manuscripts. I consider myself blessed to have found her as a partner for life and hope that I never take her for granted. Dorothy, I love you and thank you.

Our boys are not generally very enthusiastic about my pursuits with regard to the fire service, but I must thank them for patiently indulging me when we happened on a multiple alarm fire in Philadelphia during a family trip. Scott, our youngest, has of late shown an increasing interest in fire trucks. He accompanied me on recent trips to photograph trucks in several states, plus he joined me on a visit and walk-through of the Pierce facility in Appleton, Wisconsin. I am very happy to be able to share some of this with him and welcome his companionship again in the future. James, our eldest, has surprised me on several occasions by calling to let me know about fires that I'm unable to get to and keeping me up-to-date on fires that occur near the University of Illinois campus, where he attends school.

I have always considered myself fortunate to have the ability to pursue my passions, both as a hobby and through my professional career. It is truly a gift that should never be taken for granted.

Introduction

The fire service utilizes several different types of apparatus in the day-to-day duties required to protect lives and property. The most common and readily noticed rigs are pumpers and aerials. A modern history of pumpers is available in *Pumpers: Workhorse Fire Engines*, which was published by MBI Publishing Company in 1999. The book also includes a full and comprehensive study of cabs and chassis. Though many of these achievements and upgrades are touched upon in this new book, the full depth of the information is not repeated. *Aerial Fire Trucks* is intended to fulfill a similar purpose by tracing the modern evolution of aerials in the fire service. As proper terminology in the fire service refers to a pumper as an engine, an aerial unit is commonly referred to as a truck, although phraseology can differ by describing certain units as towers, quints, and Snorkels. As a means to incorporate all of the major advances in the industry, many upgrades and changes that have occurred since the pumper book was published are outlined here—even to the extent that they are not unique to aerials.

From the earliest horse-drawn and hand-drawn wooden aerial devices to the motorized apparatus that followed, this book is intended as a guide to the progression of trucks in the fire service. The historical data covered in the first chapter is a mere skimming of the fascinating beginnings for the fire service. Although this book is intended to be a modern historical accounting of aerials, some of the first accomplishments in fire fighting are included to illustrate how this equipment developed and advanced as it did. People who want more in-depth coverage on fire fighting history should explore the many books devoted to this fascinating subject.

This book includes stories that are not readily accessible to many outside the industry, plus descriptions of many one-of-a-kind aerial units. The information came from several sources, not the least of which were the men and women who actually designed, marketed, and sold these aerials.

CHAPTER ONE

A HISTORICAL REVIEW

The Early 1900s

Fire engines preceding the turn of the twentieth century were horse drawn. The fire pumps were external combustion engines, either powered by hand or by steam. Modernization followed along two lines. First, horses were replaced by internal combustion engines in the role of transporting the unit. This occurred in the first part of the 1900s. Early motorization was used to pull the existing steam pumpers and ladder trucks, since these apparatus were not past their usable life span. Seagrave is said to have introduced the first internal combustion engine for the fire service in 1906. In 1909, the first gas-powered ladder truck was sold to the fire department in Allentown, Pennsylvania, by the International Motor Company, which later became Mack Trucks. In the same year, Seagrave sold their first gas-powered, tractor-drawn, 75-foot aerial ladder. In the

mid-1910s, the leading builders of motorized fire apparatus included Ahrens Fox and names associated with modern times, such as American LaFrance, Mack, and Seagrave. Battery power competed for several years with gasoline powered engines, but proved to be slower. In addition, the battery designs often ran out of power before returning to the fire station. Christie's Front Drive Auto Company made many of the early two-wheel tractors purchased in the 1910s, which were used to pull steamers, water towers, and aerial ladders previously pulled by horses. American LaFrance offered two- and four-wheel tractors in the mid-1910s, and more motorized aerial apparatus began to appear around 1916.

The second aspect of modernization for the fire service involved the use of the internal combustion engine to power the fire pump. In some instances, the gasoline-powered fire

Bedford Park, Illinois, sits across the street from Chicago's Midway Airport. Between 1959 and 1997, they purchased three Snorkel articulating platform aerials. The first Snorkel was this 65-foot unit, built in 1959. It was one of the first units sold by Snorkel after the introduction of the Giraffe to the fire service in Chicago. Unlike the Chicago units, the Bedford Park Snorkel was built on a tandem-axle GMC chassis, and featured bodywork with storage space by Auto Body Works of Appleton, Wisconsin.

pump preceded motorized propulsion. Some pumpers drawn by hand or horses in the early 1900s had gasoline-powered fire pumps made by the Ahrens Manufacturing Company. As early as 1906, the Waterous Engine Works Company built a two-engine pumper. One engine propelled the vehicle, while the second engine ran the fire pump. American LaFrance was working to the same end in the early 1900s. In 1907, Waterous

Chicago purchased four of the German Magirus rear-mounted aerials on Mack chassis in the late 1950s. One is shown here with the aerial to the roof at a 2-11 alarm fire at 1800 Larrabee Street in April 1962. Both the Magirus and the Pirsch ladder visible in the background are set onto the building roofs for support. Early ladders were meant to be used in this fashion, unlike modern aerials, which can support several hundred pounds at any elevation while cantilevered. A Snorkel is also in use in the photo. *Photo courtesy of Warren Redick*

had built a gasoline-powered pumper with a single motor to handle both pumping and vehicle propulsion. The trend that was eventually pursued featured the same power source, both for propulsion and for pumping.

Hook and ladder rigs during the late 1800s carried many ground ladders, some of which had lengths of up to 75 feet. These were dangerous to use and often resulted in injuries to firefighters from ladders slipping. Beginning in 1868 with a design by Daniel D. Hayes, a mechanic working for the San Francisco Fire Department, there were a small number of inventions to aid the men in raising the main aerial ladder, which included anchoring the biggest ladder to a rotating turntable on the wagon bed. These designs utilized worm gears, cranks, pulleys and winches, and then compressed air pistons. In 1902, Seagrave first offered a spring-operated hoist system for raising ladders, which was later followed by Ahrens Fox, American LaFrance, Pirsch, and Mack through the 1920s and into the 1930s.

The 1920s

In the early 1920s, Pirsch, FWD, and Boyer were building tractor-drawn aerials (TDAs) in addition to Ahrens Fox, American LaFrance, Mack, and Seagrave. Most of these aerials had a reach of 75 feet. Mack first began offering aerial ladders in 1929, with 65- or 75-foot lengths. Aerial ladders during this time period were made of wood. The spring hoist mechanism required three to four men to raise the aerial. These units and the men who were assigned to them constituted a considerable amount of weight, which was quite burdensome to even the strongest horses during the years prior to the use of motorized tractors. In 1924, the German builder Magirus displayed an innovative aerial ladder in the United States. It was a rear-mounted, four-section, 85-foot aerial on a chassis that was roughly as large as a pumper. Although it did not become popular at that time, the aerial would prove to be far ahead of its time in the American aerial ladder industry. During that time period, Ward LaFrance entered the business of building fire apparatus, initially offering pumpers only.

The 1930s

In 1930, the Pirsch Company entered the aerial ladder market, and by 1931 the company built the first fully powered wooden aerial ladder that could be operated by one man. Also in the early 1930s, Ernest Maxim, whose father C. W. Maxim founded the Maxim Motor Company,

was interested in entering the aerial market. Ernest went to Europe in hopes of learning about aerial ladders overseas visiting with Magirus and Metz, two European aerial manufacturers. Also during the 1930s, Ahrens Fox introduced the first wooden aerial ladder with a nozzle at the end, combining the features of an aerial ladder with a water tower. American LaFrance, Mack, Pirsch, and Seagrave were still building wooden ladders until 1935, when Pirsch introduced the first three-section aerial ladder made of aluminum. This ladder had a length of 100 feet and its operation was fully powered. During the same time frame, Pirsch continued selling a mechanically operated ladder series in 60- and 65-foot lengths referred to as Junior Aerials, that were less expensive for fire departments. Also in 1935, Seagrave built a three-section, welded, tubular, steel aerial ladder. This was a hydraulic design with a reach of 65 feet. Pirsch continued to refine their aluminum ladder during the late 1930s. Apparatus bodies were of an open design, including the cabs, which had no doors or roofs. Ward LaFrance introduced a new design and styling for its fire apparatus chassis in 1936 with a V-shaped grille. All aerials in the industry that offered 85 feet or 100 feet of reach were tractor-drawn through the late 1930s.

Innovations continued with American LaFrance beginning production of a hydraulic, four-section, steel aerial in 1938. Also in 1938, American LaFrance changed the look of fire apparatus with the introduction of the 500 Series, which offered seating for four or five firefighters. The cabs had doors and a windshield, although most still had no roof overhead. The bodies were also being offered with enclosures for equipment storage. The 500 Series aerials were available with aerial lengths of 85 feet, 100 feet, 125 feet, and 150 feet. Another feature that was built into these tillered aerials was a new position for the tillerman's seat. Previous designs had the seat positioned over the rear of the ladder, which meant that the seat had to swing out of the way before the aerial could be raised at a fire scene. The 500 Series featured the seat past the tip of the ladder in a stationary position. In the late 1930s, Duo-Safety, a builder of ground ladders, developed a steel aerial device with the intent of offering it to any fire apparatus builder. The company ran out of money and offered Mack the first opportunity to buy the design. When Mack turned it down, the company went to Ernie Maxim, who had been looking for an aerial ladder. This was a 65-foot, three-section aerial design with a turntable and outriggers. Mack would later market this under its name in the late 1940s.

Several aerial devices are in operation at this 5-11 alarm fire in February of 1958 at Wilmot and Oakley Streets in Chicago. Visible on both sides of the building are tractor-drawn wooden aerial ladders propped up against the buildings for support. Also in use on the left side is an early water tower–elevated master stream. The firefighter rode the bucket up to his current position. He could have deployed a master stream from that position but instead chose to utilize the nozzle at the top of the extension. *Photo courtesy of Warren Redick*

The 1940s

Ahrens Fox delivered its last 85-foot TDA in 1940 to New York City. Maxim had an all-steel, hydraulic ladder for sale in the early 1940s that utilized a winch extension system. The first Maxim unit was a mid-mounted, 65-foot straight frame delivered to the Boston Fire Department. It was ready for delivery just prior to the bombing of Pearl Harbor, at which time the government froze all production and delivery of fire apparatus, and confiscated the Boston aerial. The U.S. Navy took the aerial and repainted it gray before assigning it to the Quonset Point Naval Academy, south of Providence, Rhode Island. In its haste to put the unit in service, the Navy did not sand down the Boston Fire Department lettering along the hood, and the outline of the name remained visible under the gray paint. When the Boston aerial was produced, American LaFrance and Seagrave sued Maxim for copyright infringements pertaining to the winch extension system. The lawsuits were put on hold until after the war. Ernie Maxim reportedly told lawyers for the plaintiffs that since the Navy had confiscated the aerial, they were free to sue the Navy. Maxim decided to pursue a different method for ladder extension from that point forward. Aerial ladder production was suspended until after the war ended in 1945.

Most of the larger companies were building everything for themselves including the cab, chassis, body, and aerial device. Cabs were engine-ahead designs, meaning the engine was in front of the driver and passenger compartment of the cab. Ahrens Fox produced engines for powering its own units from 1914 until the late 1920s and early 1930s. American LaFrance was one of several companies that produced its own engines beginning in 1931. Mack and Seagrave also built engines, and in the mid-1940s the companies were building large V-12s. American LaFrance introduced the 700 Series in 1946. This was the first cab-forward design for fire trucks. The driver

available in 65-, 75-, and 85-foot lengths. After the war ended and production resumed, Ernie Maxim emerged from the controversy with American LaFrance and Seagrave over the winch extension system with a newly developed hydraulic cylinder extension system. Although he was not an engineer, he was very creative in finding solutions to problems. Maxim followed American LaFrance and Seagrave in 1949 with a three-section, 75-foot aerial on a straight frame chassis (instead of tractor-drawn). After Maxim brought out these aerials, Mack re-introduced an aerial product line featuring the three sizes of Maxim ladders with bodywork by Mack.

Built in 1955, this 100-foot American LaFrance 700 Series midship aerial is an example of the first cab-forward design for fire trucks that was introduced in 1946. The driver and officer were seated at the very front of the cab with the engine placed behind them. It was offered for pumpers, quads, and city service trucks, as well as aerials with lengths ranging from 65 feet to 100 feet.

and officer were seated at the very front of the cab with the engine placed behind them. The 700 Series provided a better turning radius as well as improved visibility. It was offered for pumpers, quads, and city service trucks, as well as for aerials with lengths ranging from 65 feet to 100 feet. In the years following, Mack, Pirsch, Seagrave, and Ward LaFrance produced cab-forward designs of their own. At that time, most builders were also offering all-steel aerials with full hydraulic power. Another first for the industry came from American LaFrance—the first all-hydraulic, steel ladder that was not tractor drawn. The company produced a mid-ship-mounted, four-section, steel ladder with lengths up to 100 feet that could now rest on a two-axle, straight frame chassis, with the cab-forward design.

Along with this introduction came the emergence of other two-axle, midship aerials to compete with the traditional tractor-drawn models. Seagrave followed American LaFrance with two-axle, steel aerials that were

The 1950s

In 1950, American LaFrance produced its last wooden aerials with spring-assisted mechanisms. Pirsch was offering both two-section, wooden aerials and three-section, aluminum aerials. In 1951, Seagrave celebrated its 70th anniversary with the release of the Anniversary Series engine-ahead style and their own V-12 powerplant. Maxim began selling tractor-drawn aerials in the early 1950s and also offered an 85-foot, four-section ladder. Maxim became the sole U.S. distributor of the German Magirus, rear-mounted, four-section, steel aerial ladders in 1952. These aerials were available in lengths of 100, 144, and 170 feet, and were mounted on chassis the size of pumpers. Although several were built on Mack and other chassis, the ladders did not prove popular in the United States. Most of the approximately 20 units built between 1952 and 1964 were delivered to fire departments in Canada, mainly in the

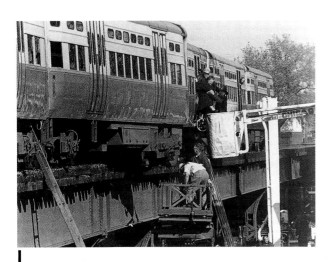

Chicago is known for the elevated train that runs around the downtown area and throughout many neighborhoods. The city needs to have the means of accessing these trains in the event of emergencies that occur above street level. In an undated photo, firefighters are shown assisting a woman from a transit authority car into the platform of an early Pitman Snorkel following a derailment. A second Snorkel is visible in the background as well as a special transit authority lift to assist train workers. *From the collection of Gary Handwerk*

province of Quebec, where European practices were common in the fire service. The small amount sold in the United States included a few to the city of Philadelphia; two 144-foot, six-section ladders to New York City; two 144-foot and two 100-foot units to Chicago; two 100-foot units to Milwaukee on Mack chassis; and a 144-foot, six-section on a Seagrave chassis to Green Bay, Wisconsin. The chassis for the Magirus units were sent to Maxim where the aerials, turntables, and stabilizers were mounted. Next, each aerial went for bodywork to the company that sold it.

Mack introduced the B-model chassis in 1954 for pumpers and aerials. This popular chassis was produced until 1967. During 1956, Seagrave purchased Maxim. Because both companies made aerial ladders and engine-ahead fire apparatus, they operated as separate companies. FWD was the only company still offering wooden aerial ladders in the mid-1950s; the City of New York Fire Department (FDNY) was possibly the last department using them. American LaFrance stopped producing its gas engines in 1955. In that same year, Ward LaFrance began offering 65-foot, 75-foot, and 85-foot ladders from Maxim in both straight-frame and tractor-drawn configurations. Also in 1955, Seagrave created a lighter weight, lower cost, 65-foot steel aerial that could be mounted on a commercial chassis, which gave smaller departments the ability to

purchase a ladder truck. Seagrave also offered a midship-mounted, four-section, 85-foot aerial.

In 1956, American LaFrance upgraded the 700 Series and announced the 800 Series. This new cab and chassis offered additional options for the engine type, along with cosmetic styling changes. During the same year, FWD became the U.S. distributor of the Geesink ladder built by a Dutch company. This was a line of rear-mounted, steel aerials that were offered in lengths of 65, 75, 85, and 107 feet.

In 1957, Mack began selling its new cab-forward C-model line for pumpers, city service trucks, and aerials including tractor-drawn ladders. During this time period, manufacturers began introducing commercial chassis for the fire service as a less expensive option to the custom chassis built by the apparatus builders. Ford introduced the C-Series in 1957, which became extremely popular with the fire service. Pirsch and Seagrave both offered aerials on Ford chassis that were considered relatively inexpensive when matched with the custom chassis. Ward LaFrance redesigned its custom chassis in 1957, offering a rounded hood and flat grille.

American LaFrance joined other aerial builders in 1958 when it began to offer 65-foot and 75-foot three-section aerials on commercial chassis. American LaFrance also unveiled a completely restyled 900 Series with a wider cab, smooth, rounded front, and bigger windshield. Seagrave released a new 100-foot, four-section, midship-mounted, steel aerial on a four-wheel chassis, and Maxim added a 100-foot TDA to its product line.

At the end of the 1950s, several new aerial devices were introduced into the fire service. Pitman Manufacturing of Grandview, Missouri, was building hydraulic cranes, digger derricks, and an articulated boom device with a bucket at the end called the Giraffe. Commonly referred to as a cherry picker, this device was most popular for tree trimming although it was also used by the military for de-icing and decontamination tasks. The design concept had been licensed to Pitman from a Canadian company that developed an articulating device, which was originally mounted on a trailer pulled behind another vehicle. This unit was designed for picking apples (and by rights should have been called an apple picker instead of a cherry picker). Ray Schuster of Illinois FWD, the Chicago area dealer for Pitman, was a supplier of fire engines and utility vehicles to the City of Chicago. He had a green and yellow, demonstrator, 50-foot, articulated boom truck that was

An extra alarm fire in Chicago in the fall of 1959 required the deployment of several aerial devices. In the foreground is an early Pirsch tractor-drawn aerial. Visible toward the rear of the unit is the tillerman's seat, which was swung to the side to allow the ladder to be raised. Three different Quinn Snorkels are applying elevated master streams to the buildings. Two units are Hi-Ranger Snorkels and one is a Pitman Snorkel. Chicago purchased the Hi-Ranger units when they were offered for less money than the Pitman units. *Photo courtesy of Warren Redick*

outfitted for tree trimming. It had a steel cage cover over the top of the cab and hood to prevent damage from falling tree limbs. He invited representatives from the parks department to view the product. A gentleman by the name of Ed Prendergast from the Chicago Fire Department, who was responsible for apparatus procurement and the repair shops, came along too. The Chicago Fire Department was eager to replace its 30-year-old water towers at that time. After viewing the Pitman 50-foot Giraffe, he asked to borrow it for some experiments with regards to the fire service. He took it back to the fire department shops and strapped a traditional fire hose along the boom sections up to the bucket. Then he took a street-level deluge gun and wired it into the bucket to find out if this boom could handle the backpressure from the charged nozzle. He found that it would handle all of the nozzle pressure for whatever water could be pumped through it. The truck impressed Fire Commissioner Robert Quinn, who had also seen Giraffes working with a major outdoor sign company. He was very interested in performing further testing. The Giraffe was still painted green and yellow when it was sent to a Still and Box alarm fire at a grocery store near the corner of 27th and State Streets one evening and put to work for the first time.

When Ray Schuster called the shops some days later to see if the department was done experimenting with his demonstrator, he was told that the unit was stationed at a busy firehouse running to all extra-alarm fires. The trial was successful, but the fire department wanted it to be fitted with a permanent pipe and proper monitor. The unit went back to Pitman, where workers fitted a 3-inch aluminum pipe along one side of the boom all the way to the bucket. An Akron monitor nozzle was installed that offered 180 degrees of lateral swing in addition to vertical adjustments, and the bucket was enlarged slightly to enhance rescue capabilities. The truck had been painted red and black with a white boom and became the first articulated water tower purchased by Chicago. This first unit was followed closely by a second.

Early in the summer of 1958, Art Moore, a minority partner in Pitman Manufacturing, which was handling sales of the unit, was in Chicago chasing the unit to fires and observing its use. He glanced at a Sunday newspaper and noticed a headline that read, "Quinn's Snorkel the Hottest Thing in Firefighting." He had been looking for a name for this new product and was intrigued by what he read. The accompanying article recalled an interview with the firefighters who had used the aerial at a fire scene. They had been involved with going from window to window, pouring water on the fire. As they moved between the windows, the stream of water hit the solid walls and splashed back to drench them. The firefighters had been calling it Quinn's Snorkel. The reporter remarked that a snorkel was a device to be used under water, and the firefighters asked the reporter where he thought they'd just been. Promptly, Art Moore had a trademark search done on the name "snorkel"

Norwood Park, Illinois, owned this midship, 85-foot, 1961 Maxim aerial mounted on a Mack C-model chassis. Mack was a distributor of the Maxim aerials for several years. The box along the ladder contained a large saw to cut roof holes for ventilation.

The long rear overhang on this 100-foot, midship-mounted 1962 Pirsch aerial presented considerable challenges for the driver. Firefighters who did not fit inside the conventional cab rode on the step at the rear of the unit.

and registered it for the product. This was the birth of the Pitman Snorkel. Moore recognized the potential in the fire service application of this product. He sold his interest in Pitman and founded the Snorkel Fire Equipment Company, which at the time was strictly a sales company contracting with Pitman for manufacturing. On the first of December in 1958, a tragic fire broke out at the Our Lady of the Angels school in Chicago. The Snorkel was one of the units sent to the fire scene and put to work performing rescue and fire suppression duties.

Moore needed to have a complete package so he could market the Snorkel to other fire departments. He made a deal with Doug Ogilvie of Auto Body Works in Appleton, Wisconsin, to fabricate bodies for the Snorkel. The first body design concept was drawn on a cocktail napkin during a dinner meeting between Moore and Ogilvie. A 65-foot Snorkel with compartments by Auto Body Works on a Ford chassis was displayed at the 1959 International Association of Fire-Chiefs (IAFC) convention in Grand Rapids, Michigan. After touring from coast to coast making demonstrations, it was sold to the fire department in Elwood, Indiana, late in 1960. There were four main chassis available for the Snorkel—the Ford C-Series, the International CO8190, an FWD, and an Oshkosh chassis. All but the Ford were offered with five-man custom canopy cabs for the fire service.

Later that same year, a company called Mobil Aerial Towers offered the Hi-Ranger, another articulating device with a platform at the end, to compete with Snorkel. Unlike the Snorkel's solid boom, the Hi-Ranger had an open, lattice-style boom design. The Chicago Fire Department purchased several Hi-Ranger platforms that were offered on a lower bid, but the Pitman Snorkel was better suited to the fire service and became a popular item with fire departments across the country. Chicago later replaced its Hi-Rangers with Snorkel units.

In 1959, Mack sold 13 Maxim aerials to the FDNY all on C-85 tractors. Two were four-section, 100-foot units and the other 11 were 85-foot tractor-drawn models. The 11 TDAs featured trailer frames built by Mack instead of Maxim. The ladders, turntables, and outriggers for these aerials came from Maxim with the wooden ground ladders. The 100-foot units were unique rigs since Maxim did not yet offer a four-section, 100-foot ladder of its own. Instead, these units featured a Maxim turntable and stabilizers with Magirus ladder sections. These hybrids were stronger than the conventional Magirus 100-foot units since the FDNY aerials were built with the bottom four sections from the 144-foot, six-section aerial, and were wider and stronger than most. The Magirus 100-foot

ladder was built with the top four sections of the 144-foot ladder. The reasoning behind the design of these special 100-foot units for New York City was that the Magirus turntable was very high which required the pedestal to be mounted very low. Interestingly enough, the Magirus aerial pedestal was actually developed for World War II as the pedestal for the German 88-millimeter howitzer artillery gun, which accounted for the high design. When used in the fire service, this design provided a minimum of storage for equipment and little space for ground ladders that were an integral part of the fire service in the United States.

Aerial units were used differently in Europe; they were lighter in design and had lower tip load capacities. In

The Oakbrook Terrace Fire Protection District, formerly known as the Butterfield Fire Protection District, owned this 1964 Snorkel. The 85-foot model always required a tandem-axle chassis to support the weight when it had a pump and water tank. Early 85-foot Snorkels without a pump and tank were built on single-axle chassis and had a very long front overhang. Because the Ford was a popular option for customers who wanted a commercial chassis, the conventional GMC chassis was used much less often. This unit had a 1,000 gallon-per-minute pump and carried 200 gallons of water. Shortly after this unit was delivered, Snorkel operations left Pitman Manufacturing and subsequent units no longer carried the Pitman prefix to the Snorkel logo.

Europe, the units were called "escapes," and were meant for use as a means to escape a building. They were not used as ladder pipes or water towers, and they had very limited reach at low elevations. The Maxim turntable allowed for a more conventional body design, maximum utilization of the body for the fire department, and the additional ladder capabilities required in U.S. fire departments. The Maxim pedestal was adapted to the Magirus ladder sections until Maxim was able to produce its own 100-foot, four-section ladder in 1960.

Maxim introduced its custom cab-forward model F design in 1959. That same year, FWD brought out its cab-forward design and Seagrave released a cab-forward design as well. Seagrave also discontinued the lighter weight aerial for commercial chassis and began mounting the standard aerials on both custom and commercial chassis.

Nineteen fifty-nine was also the year that the Sutphen Corporation, a company that had been producing pumpers since 1949, began to contemplate an elevated platform aerial. Sutphen was a distributor for Pirsch aerials,

complementing its own line of pumpers since the late 1940s. Tom Sutphen viewed the articulating elevated platform devices and was interested in improving on the horizontal reach capabilities for fire departments. Working with an aluminum engineer from ALCOA, the company began the design process for a telescopic, elevated-platform aerial built from aluminum. The concept included utilizing bolts instead of welds. Learning from the construction of airplanes, high-rise buildings, and bridges that were bolted together, Sutphen felt that when the aluminum alloy was hot enough to be welded it would loose tensil strength and lower the yield point, which could make the metal susceptible to cracking. The first prototype of this aerial would be completed in the early 1960s.

Also in 1959, Grove Manufacturing of Shady Grove, Pennsylvania, began to experiment with an aerial ladder for the fire service. Two brothers who were farmers started Grove several years earlier. Working for themselves, they had built a wagon that was noticed by others, who then asked the brothers to build wagons for them. One

In 1966, Oakbrook, Illinois, received the fourth tower built by Sutphen with shop number HS412. This was an 85-foot unit, with a 228-inch wheelbase on a single-axle International CO8191 chassis with a Cincinnati Cab. Sutphen built less than 20 units on single-axle chassis before adopting the tandem axles, although several of the original 20 were 65- and 75-foot units. This truck had a five-speed manual transmission, a 285-horsepower 549 FS gasoline-powered engine, and a 1,000-gallon-per-minute Barton American pump. When Oakbrook replaced this unit in 1988, it was sold to the Community Fire Company in North Grosvenordle, Connecticut.

Several companies entered into the articulating aerial market that was pioneered by Snorkel. In 1963, Seagrave worked with a company in Ohio to buy an exclusive articulating aerial device. Offered initially as a two-boom design, it was then built as a three-boom unit with a reach of 90 feet. Marketed as the Eagle by Seagrave, the device was called the Strato-Tower by the fabricator. Melrose Park, Illinois, took delivery in 1966 of this 90-foot Eagle unit on a custom Seagrave chassis with a 1,000-gallon-per-minute pump. It used two pair of hydraulic A-style jacks for support.

process in wagon production required the unit to be flipped over. The Grove brothers designed and built a crane to accomplish this task. Others again noticed the brothers' useful device and asked them to reproduce the crane. Grove Manufacturing thus pursued the business of building cranes, farm wagons, bale bodies, and later, forage bodies. The Grove fire service aerial ladders emerged as a natural progression from the cranes and shared several components. Common elements were the hydraulic system, elevation cylinders, outrigger stabilization design, and the turntable rotation. Grove used a chain extension system for the ladder sections, which the trade would later affectionately call a bicycle chain extension. Grove's original aerial for the fire service was a 65-foot ladder with a steel base section, and aluminum middle and fly sections. The first unit of this style went to Mexico, Missouri. Only two or three others were built this way.

The 1960s

In 1960, Maxim developed a four-section, 100-foot aerial, and stopped using the Magirus ladder, although the company continued as a Magirus distributor into the mid-1960s. The Maxim ladder was a mid-mount design that was also offered as a tiller. At that time, the Maxim aerial line consisted of the three-section 65-foot, and four-section 85-foot, mid-mount ladders. The four-section 100-foot was a light-duty ladder similar to those offered throughout the industry. Use of the aerial had restrictions with a man at the tip and the ladder at low elevations, because extension was restricted to approximately 50 feet with a 200-pound man at the tip. Maxim delivered an additional 13 85-foot tractor-drawn aerials to New York City making a total of 26 units in two years. FDNY also bought 13 American LaFrance 100-foot TDAs with steel ladders at the same time. Also in 1960, Auto Body Works, Inc., of Appleton, Wisconsin, became Pierce Auto Body Works.

Snorkel allowed its name to be registered for use by the Hi-Ranger from Mobil Aerial Towers and by Simon Engineering, a company from Dudley, England, that was also building an articulated boom platform device. The Hi-Ranger Snorkel and Simon Snorkel products were offered to fire departments and had nothing to do with Snorkel Fire Equipment or Pitman Manufacturing. In the early 1960s, Snorkel Fire Equipment added an 85-foot Snorkel to the line.

Pirsch introduced the Safety Cab in 1961 with the company's trademark flat-nosed cab-forward design. Seagrave introduced a four-section, steel aerial for its tractor-drawn units. Differing from the three-section models, the four-section had a fixed seat for the tillerman that did not have to move for aerial operation. With Seagrave's and most

Wilmette, Illinois, was a loyal Seagrave customer for many years. At one time its two stations had a total of three Seagrave pumpers, a ladder, and a Snorkel with a Seagrave chassis. The ladder was a 100-foot, 1962 midship quint with a 1,000 gallon-per-minute pump and 300-gallon water tank. The P-Series cab-forward design was introduced in 1959.

other builders' three-section designs, the tillerman's seat rested on top of the ladder sections and needed to be swung out of the way before operating the ladder. In 1961, with the continued and growing popularity of the Snorkel devices, Seagrave offered 65-foot and 85-foot two-section articulating platform models on its chassis.

Also in 1961, Sutphen completed its first 65-foot, three-section, all-aluminum, midship-mounted, telescopic elevated platform, on a Ford C-950 Series chassis. Powered by a gasoline engine, this unit had a pump, 300 gallons of water, and was built on a single-axle pumper chassis. It had a waterway running to the tip that led to a patented system featuring a yoke and dual turrets on either side of the platform. The 65-foot unit sold for $39,500. The first unit

toured the country as a demonstrator for several years before Sutphen sold it to the fire department in Norwalk, Ohio, in 1964. During the design process for the 65-foot tower, Sutphen worked on a 24-foot, two-section aerial and a 35-foot unit. Both of these prototype aerials featured the same box boom design, but neither was ever completed.

In 1962, Ward LaFrance released a cab-forward design called the Mark I, later renamed the P-80. The company also became the principal distributor of the Hi-Ranger Snorkels. These were built on the custom cab-forward P-80 chassis that were later changed to the Ambassador Series. The largest models utilized a modified lower profile cab to reduce the travel height. The first Ward LaFrance Hi-Ranger was delivered in September of 1962 to the fire department in

GROVE MANUFACTURING COMPANY
DIVISION OF WALTER KIDDE & CO., INC.
GREENCASTLE, PENNSYLVANIA 17225

4S-100' ALL-STEEL HYDRAULIC AERIAL LADDER
FULLY-EXTENDED, UNSUPPORTED OVER THE REAR
SHOWN BEARING THE WEIGHT OF A CAR AND THE
ASSOCIATED RIGGING DURING A LIFTING TEST.

These are early Grove promotional photos illustrating the strength of the 4S-100 steel ladder. Pictured below is the entire manufacturing staff for the fire ladder division, plus a few other plant workers. *From the collection of Gary Handwerk*

GROVE MANUFACTURING COMPANY
DIVISION OF WALTER KIDDE & CO., INC.
GREENCASTLE, PENNSYLVANIA 17225

4S-100' ALL-STEEL HYDRAULIC AERIAL LADDER
FULLY-EXTENDED, UNSUPPORTED OVER THE REAR
DEMONSTRATING UNUSUAL STRUCTURAL RIGIDITY
AND STRENGTH BEARING THE WEIGHT OF 8 MEN.
WITH THIS LOADING THE LADDER WAS ELEVATED
AND LOWERED, EXTENDED AND RETRACTED. THIS
WAS PURELY A TEST. REFER TO SPECIFICATION
SHEET FOR STANDARD OPERATION LOAD RATINGS.

Bristol, Rhode Island. Also in 1962, American LaFrance unveiled an articulating platform aerial called the Aero-Chief. This two-piece boom design was initially offered as a 70-foot model; the company added 80-foot and 90-foot versions in 1963. The original demo unit that was sold to Berkeley, California, in 1964 had a different boom design than production units featured afterward. The newer design had a top boom

that nested into the lower boom to reduce the travel height. The original design had two larger booms. Aero-Chief units that were built between 1962 and 1964 used two pair of hydraulic A-style jacks that were replaced in 1965 with two pair of radial arm jacks. The Aero-Chief could be built on a single or tandem axle chassis with or without a pump and water tank, although the quint units required the use of a tandem axle because of the added weight. Seagrave introduced a 90-foot, three-boom, articulating elevated aerial platform in 1963 that they called the Eagle. Seagrave did not build the device, which was manufactured for Seagrave of Columbus, Ohio, by the Truck and Construction Equipment Division, Paul Hardeman and Company of Bowling Green, Ohio. The fabricator referred to the device as a Strato-Tower, model S3B-90HDF with a 700-pound rated capacity. The mid-ship turntable differed from the other articulated aerials being offered at that time, and stabilization was achieved with

two pair of hydraulic A-style jacks. Only a few of the three-boom Eagle devices were eventually produced, in addition to a one of a kind, 70-foot, two-boom unit with a tubular design, which was delivered to Nashville, Tennessee, in 1963. By the end of the 1960s, after selling roughly 26 units to the fire service, the Hi-Ranger Snorkel, another competitor of the original Snorkel, was discontinued.

In the early 1960s, years after the Magirus rear-mounted aerials proved unpopular, several American manufacturers began offering rear-mounted styles. Seagrave announced the Rear Admiral aerial in 1963. It was a rear-mounted, steel aerial on a single-axle chassis. Also in 1963, FWD purchased Seagrave, moving all operations to their current home in Wisconsin, which delayed production of the Rear Admiral unit.

In 1963, Pirsch began to offer hydraulic jacks as an option, followed by Seagrave a year later. Also, a one of a

Ward LaFrance was an early OEM with Grove. This is a 1968 midship-mounted ladder from the North Maine Fire Protection District in Illinois. Built on an Ambassador chassis, the 4S-100 ladder carried a serial number of 210768. The fire department had two matching Ward LaFrance Ambassador pumpers.

kind, two-boom articulating elevated platform was built by Seagrave with a reach of 70 feet. During the same time, Don Smeal was designing and building equipment relating to various agricultural industries when he was approached by the local volunteer fire department in Snyder, Nebraska, to repair the water tank in a pumper. He instead suggested that the fire department buy a new chassis and allow him to fabricate a body for them that would include an aerial ladder. The unique unit that he built, which would prove to be years ahead of its time, featured a fully-enclosed area for the crew, plus a 42-foot, two-section, steel, hydraulic aerial ladder. This unit was stabilized by one set of rear A-style jacks and could support 400 pounds at the tip. This was the only 42-foot aerial ladder built by Smeal. Snyder, with a population near 300, may have been the smallest community in America with a ladder truck. Neighboring departments began calling on Smeal to build apparatus for them after viewing the rig he had fabricated, and Smeal was

Morton Grove, a suburb of Chicago, painted its rigs in the traditional Chicago black-over-red color scheme. The city had a fleet of custom Pirsch apparatus, including this 85-foot, 1967 midship-mounted aerial ladder with a custom safety cab. The chrome handrail decorating the top rear of the cab would prove in later years to be a costly addition to the Pirsch rigs. A disabling accident occurred when a firefighter lost his grip while standing as the rig was in motion. A court found Pirsch negligent for installing the handrail, which encouraged him to stand instead of remaining seated. The costly settlement was one of the major factors in the eventual demise of the company.

in the fire apparatus business from that point forward. Between 1963 and 1969, Smeal built three-section, 65-foot aerial ladders for Crete, Chadron, West Point, and Plattsmouth, Nebraska.

In 1964 Mack engineered a brand-new product in response to requests from FDNY chiefs for a new aerial device. Commonly referred to as a tower ladder, it was a hydraulic, 75-foot, mid-mounted, solid boom design, telescoping aerial with a platform at the end and a pre-piped waterway. It also had an escape ladder along the top of the boom. This was known as the Aerialscope. Mack gave a contract to the Eaton Metal Company in Denver to build the Aerialscope. The original product was constructed with the cylinder and water system inside the enclosed box boom. First models were offered on the Mack C-model chassis and powered by gasoline engines.

By 1964, Grove had built 13 aerial ladders for the fire service. To put into perspective the aerial production versus cranes, Grove was averaging one ladder every 6 weeks and 275 cranes per month. The ladders were built, painted, and mounted by hand. Four men and a band saw plus two welders handled all production. Early customers included the John Bean Company, Ward LaFrance, Howe, and Barton American, which was the biggest customer.

Also in 1964, Pitman Manufacturing was experiencing production complications due to its Snorkel manufacturing. The units took longer to complete and were considerably larger than the products Pitman was selling. As a result, Snorkel Fire Equipment acquired the inventory from Pitman, along with their chief engineer, and moved production to St. Joseph, Missouri, where they took over sales and manufacturing of the aerial devices. Snorkel began operations on December 28, 1964, and the Pitman Snorkel became the Snorkel. Production rose to 15 units per month after the introduction of the 75-foot Snorkel in 1965.

Ward LaFrance introduced the P-82 Series custom cab-forward chassis design in 1965. Compared to the P-80 Series, this was a more conventional curved cab design and it proved to be considerably more popular with fire departments.

Also in 1965, the first production model of the Sutphen elevated platform, known as the Sutphen Tower, was built on a Duplex chassis and sold to the fire department in Coshocton, Ohio. This unit had a three-section, 85-foot aerial. First offered on commercial chassis from Ford or GMC, Sutphen began relying on International chassis with Cincinnati Cabs in the mid-1960s. Sutphen produced a three-section, 75-foot

This is an 85-foot, 1968 Sutphen mid-mount aerial platform from Wheeling, Illinois. The box boom design provides a protective housing for the waterway, which leads to dual guns, one on each side of the platform. Sutphen was using chassis from International with TCM Cincinnati cabs until 1972, when the company began to build its own chassis.

tower in 1966 for Parma Heights, Ohio, on a single-axle International chassis with a cab-forward Cincinnati Cab. Approximately 20 units with lengths of 65, 75, or 85 feet were produced on single axles before Sutphen adopted the tandem-axle design on the 85-foot model to ease wear and tear on the brakes and better distribute the 27,000-pound rear axle weight. Prior to that time, aerial towers in the industry were either an articulating style with a solid boom design like the Snorkel, or lattice type like the Hi-Ranger, or telescoping with a solid boom like Aerialscope. The Sutphen boom was a lattice style, box boom design that was telescopic instead of articulating. While the early Sutphen units were gas powered, several companies including Mack and American LaFrance began using more economical diesel engines around 1965.

In 1966, ATO, Inc., purchased American LaFrance. ATO was the tickertape symbol on the New York Stock Exchange for the Automatic Sprinkler Company. In 1967, the Crown Firecoach Company, a West Coast apparatus manufacturer, added aerials to its product mix. The company contracted with Maxim for midship and tractor-drawn models. Turntables, trailer frame

assemblies, and ladders were trailered across the country for assembly in Los Angeles. Mack introduced three new chassis to the fire service in 1967. The CF replaced the C, the R model conventional replaced the B model, and the flat-nosed MB was a new item. Seagrave, now part of FWD, released the 100-foot Rear Admiral aerial ladder with a short overall length. It was also offered with four-wheel drive and four-wheel steering on an FWD chassis for greater maneuverability.

In the late 1960s, Mack found a manufacturing company called Baker Equipment that was building telescopic equipment for Boeing in addition to making bucket trucks. Mack contracted with Baker to build the Aerialscope from that point forward. Once Baker began production, every Aerialscope was mounted on a CF chassis with a diesel engine. The first Baker Aerialscope was purchased by the fire department in Bedford, Ohio, while most of the others went to the FDNY. These were 75-foot

Ward LaFrance was the principal distributor for the Hi-Ranger Snorkels. Most were mounted on a low-profile P-80 or Ambassador Series chassis, including this unit built in 1966 for South Chicago Heights, Illinois.

units built on single-axle chassis with no pump. Mack sent the chassis to Baker where the tower, substructure, and body were mounted. The unit then returned to Mack for painting. When the FDNY began to take delivery of the CF models, the gasoline-powered C-model units were retired.

By 1966, Grove was building hydraulic aerial ladders for the fire service with lengths of 65, 75, 85, and 100 feet. To allow additional space for cranes in Shady Grove, the company moved aerial production from one stall of the farm division building to an old potato chip factory in Greencastle, Pennsylvania. Since the fire division was such a small portion of total Grove production, the fabrication was constantly being moved to different areas of the building to accommodate other products. When aerial orders were slow, the workers were assigned to other duties in the farm or crane divisions.

Almost any builder could market the Grove aerials and several had Original Equipment Manufacture (OEM) agreements, but the principal distributor for several years became Ward LaFrance. One of the first Ward LaFrance three-section, 65-foot Grove ladders was sold to the Dallas, Texas, fire department in October of 1966. Although Grove was located in Pennsylvania, most of the units produced in the late 1960s were purchased by fire departments in Texas including Dallas, Houston, Ft. Worth, and San Antonio, due to the strength of the distributor for that area. The majority of these were 65-, 75-, and 85-foot ladders, with two 100-foot models going to Houston in 1969.

American LaFrance offered the four-section, rear-mounted, 100-foot Ladder-Chief aerial in 1969 and began the Chief series of aerial products. At the same time, Pirsch released a rear-mounted, 100-foot, four-section, aluminum ladder. Both of these companies built the rear-mounted aerials on single-axle chassis. Seagrave's Rear Admiral was available in 65-, 75-, 85-, and 100-foot models. Maxim modified the "S" cab in 1969, replacing the steel front end with fiberglass.

The Snorkel could be ordered in 50-, 65-, 75-, and 85-foot working heights. The aerial device was built and mounted on a chassis, which was then driven to a body builder for completion. Another company that emerged into the fire service due to the popularity of the original Pitman

This is a 90-foot 1969 American LaFrance Aero-Chief articulating platform aerial from Elgin, Illinois. The open cab is a 900 Series unit and the truck has no pump or water tank. American LaFrance aerials utilized two sets of radial arm jacks surrounding the rear-mounted turntable for the 100-foot Ladder-Chief, 100-foot Water-Chief, and the Aero-Chief units.

Snorkel was the Calavar Corporation. Calavar offered the Firebird platform aerial beginning in 1969 with the ability to reach 90, 100, and 125 feet. A 150-foot model followed a few years later. Similar to other articulating platform aerials, the Firebird had a platform at the end and a two-piece solid boom style with an articulating knuckle joint between the booms. The unique feature of this aerial was that the boom sections also had the capability to telescope for additional reach. The upper boom would telescope on the 125-foot model, while both booms would extend on the 150-foot unit. The design of this aerial required four outriggers and a front-mounted downrigger for stabilization, lifting the entire truck off the ground when deployed. In order for the turntable to rotate, the ladders that were stored on the sides of the unit had to be lowered out of the way. In 1980, Calavar ceased fire service operations and pursued other markets for their products. It seemed that other articulating aerial platform manufacturers could not match Snorkel's popularity. Pierce Auto Body Works became Pierce Manufacturing in 1969, and was still the principal subcontractor providing bodywork for Snorkels sold through Snorkel Fire Equipment. By the late 1960s, the popularity of the American LaFrance Aero-Chief had grown, and accounted for roughly 15 percent of the articulated platform market, capturing a significant share of Snorkel's market.

In 1968, Snorkel Fire Equipment introduced the Squrt. This was a 54-foot, two-section, articulating water tower with a hydraulically operated, remote controlled nozzle. The Squrt was incorporated into a standard pumper body. The unit had no capability to support a person, and did not require the use of stabilizers. Standard controls were at the rear of the pumper, at the base of the Squrt pedestal. During that same time, the sales manager from Snorkel left the company to join Seagrave, in hopes of bringing another product to the market that would compete with the Snorkel articulating platform aerial. This would be the second product that Seagrave would initiate to compete with Snorkel. When he left Snorkel, the sales manager sold his shares of company stock back to Art Moore. Seagrave then contracted with Trump, Ltd. of Canada to build the new device under the model name of the Astro-Tower. Trump was the company that originally developed the articulating product before licensing the technology to Pitman Manufacturing in the late 1950s. The new venture did not result in a product coming to market, and lasted for a very short time. After it was scrapped, the sales manager left Seagrave and returned to work at Snorkel, minus his company stock.

CHAPTER TWO

THE

1970s

American Fire Apparatus

American Fire Apparatus Company of Battle Creek, Michigan, offered a little known product called the Aqua-Jet. It was a hydraulically actuated telescoping water tower that was mounted to a conventional pumper. A builder of pumpers and tankers for many years, American Fire was very popular with smaller departments in many states. The company announced the Aqua-Jet in 1972, and it was available in lengths of 55 feet or 75 feet. These aerials consisted of either a two-section or three-section telescoping box-boom with an automatic nozzle at the tip. Models were available to mount at the rear of a pumper or midship. The Aqua-Jet utilized four H-style outriggers for support with a 12-foot or 16-foot spread. It was also available with a tele-scoping rescue ladder mounted along the boom, which could be disengaged allowing the boom to extend with the waterway only, to penetrate tight areas. The majority of the 15–20 total Aqua-Jets produced were 55-foot models, and it is believed that only one or two were 75-foot units.

American was an OEM selling Grove aerial products in that company's early days, and later sold the products of Ladder Towers, Inc. (LTI). American Pump, owned by the same people as American Fire Apparatus, fabricated the telescoping tube assemblies for roughly 300 LTI waterways before pricing themselves out of the business causing LTI to begin fabricating their own.

American LaFrance

In 1970, American LaFrance introduced the 1000 Series, which offered upgrades from the 900 Series, including styling changes and standard equipment features that had been options on the prior series. In the mid-1960s, American

The Pirsch Safety Cab was constructed over a big frame by a single German craftsman and was sought after by loyal customers across the country. This 1971, four-section, 100-foot, rear-mounted aerial utilized a tandem-axle chassis. The aerial was capable of resting on a single-axle chassis when ordered without a pump and water tank. Body designs and compartment layouts were customized for each fire department.

Introducing THE AQUA-JET
A Hydraulically Actuated Telescoping Water Tower

- **EXCLUSIVE AQUA-JET MONITOR**
  Roll of 360° in a plane perpendicular to the center line of the boom. Swing 280° in a plane in line with the center line of the boom. Both motions controlled by push buttons on the operator's panel. The Roll and Swing can be operated separately or simultaneously.

- **NOZZLE**
  Features fog or straight stream with a complete range of operation from 350 gpm to 1000 gpm. Operator can actuate any pattern desired by merely pushing a button on the operator's panel.

- **EASE OF OPERATION**
  A complete push-button operation which incorporates the latest electro-hydraulic function control system. With this system, operator's panel may be placed anywhere the purchaser desires on his particular piece of apparatus. The AQUA-JET is available in various lengths.

- **OPTIMUM PRODUCTIVITY OF MANPOWER**
  Because of its compact design, the AQUA-JET can be used in confined area in which other types of booms would not operate. The AQUA-JET is designed to be used by any size fire department — from the smallest volunteer to the largest paid department — can be trained to operate the AQUA-JET in just a matter of minutes.

- **OPTIONAL (Exclusive)** . . . Remote Control . . . Radio Control

American
FIRE APPARATUS COMPANY   Battle Creek, Michigan and Marshalltown, Iowa

This sales sheet describes one of the first Aqua-Jet products that was marketed by the American Fire Apparatus Company. This early unit did not feature the rescue ladder, nor did it require jacks for stability during operations.

When ATO purchased Snorkel, several new product designations were added to the Chief Series line. A Tele-Squrt added to a pumper was designated a Duo Chief. This 1973 unit featured a Pioneer II Series chassis and a 50-foot Tele-Squrt device. The Pioneer offered great visibility with the flat, one-piece windshield, but never approached the traditional contoured series American LaFrance cabs in popularity.

LaFrance had introduced a lower cost, no-frills custom chassis called the Pioneer that was strictly for pumpers. The Pioneer received cosmetic enhancements in 1970, and in 1972, American LaFrance introduced another cab and chassis called the Pacemaker Series. This series featured an American LaFrance chassis with a Cincinnati Cab. The Pacemaker was a step up from the low-cost Pioneer Series, while not as expensive as the custom 900 or 1000 Series, and could be specified with any of the available aerial devices.

The totally redesigned Century Series superceded the 1000 Series in 1973. The cabs featured a wider, contoured front with greater visibility. In addition, the cab sides behind the driver and officer were flared out to provide even more room for the jump seat area.

In 1971, ATO, American LaFrance's parent company, purchased Snorkel Fire Equipment, expanding the American LaFrance product line even further with the Tele-Squrt, Squrt, and the Snorkel. At that time, American LaFrance discontinued the Aero-Chief articulating platform aerial. New models emerged incorporating the Snorkel products

Most of the American LaFrance Aero-Chief articulating platforms featured open cab apparatus to minimize the travel height. This unit was built in 1971 and features a 1000 Series cab and chassis. When this fire occurred, the Aero-Chief was 24 years old. It is common for aerial apparatus to be used for 20 to 30 years of service when they are properly cared for and maintained. One modern addition to the 24-year-old unit in the image is the square box on the cab, underneath the windshield. It is an optical device to trigger traffic signals, increasing safety for the crew when responding to an emergency.

into the American LaFrance line. Adding a Tele-Squrt to a pumper produced a Duo Chief, adding a Squrt yielded an Aqua Chief, and a 50-foot Snorkel mounted on a basic pumper was called a Super Chief Junior. Larger Snorkel booms mounted on truck chassis were not given a "Chief" designation. The Snorkel line continued to be available to non–American LaFrance customers. In 1973, the Pioneer Series was upgraded to accommodate all of the aerial products. Aerials could then be ordered with the Pioneer, Pacemaker, or Century Series cabs.

Another aerial was added to the product line in 1975. The Ladder-Chief was fitted with a pre-piped waterway to the tip. This new variation was called the Water-Chief, as a straight truck configuration. A Water-Chief with a pump and tank added was called a Water-Chief Quint.

Throughout the 1980s, the American LaFrance aerial product line consisted of the Mid-Ship Aerial, Mid-Ship Aerial Quint, Ladder-Chief, Ladder-Chief Quint, Water-Chief, Water-Chief Quint, TDAs, and the Snorkel products. The Mid-Ship Aerials and Mid-Ship Aerial Quints differed in that the quints had an American LaFrance Twinflow pump of 1,000 to 2,000 gallons per minute, plus a 300-gallon water tank. The 100-foot, four-section steel ladders required two jacks with a 12-foot spread. Manually operated jacks were standard with an option for hydraulic A-style jacks. The quint had slightly less compartment space than the straight ladder.

The Ladder-Chief featured a rear-mounted, four-section, 100-foot, steel ladder on a single-axle chassis. Adding dual

The tractor-drawn aerial also used a 100-foot, four-section, steel ladder. No quint option or pre-piped waterway was available. Stabilization required four manually operated jacks positioned amidships around the turntable, requiring 16 feet of clearance. Standard for all of the aerial bodies was galvaneal steel with an upgrade to stainless steel as an option.

This is a 1977 American LaFrance Century Series Water-Chief Quint. It has a pre-piped waterway to differentiate it from a Ladder-Chief and is a quint because of the 1,500 gallon-per-minute pump and 300-gallon water tank. The tandem axle was a requirement for the quint, due to the added weight of the pump and water tank. American LaFrance placed both sets of radial arm jacks at the rear of the unit, unlike other builders, who placed one set toward the cab.

pre-piped waterways that ran along the outside of the aerial to a Ladder-Chief changed the designation to a Water-Chief. All other characteristics were the same. By adding a Twinflow pump and a 200-gallon water tank to a Ladder-Chief, the model would be a Ladder-Chief Quint, and adding the pre-piped waterway again altered the product to a Water-Chief Quint. The 100-foot Ladder-Chief and Water-Chief models all required four A-style jacks that were hydraulically operated. Ladder-Chief and Water-Chief models were set on single-axle chassis, while the addition of fire pumps and water tanks required tandem axles. Standard ground-ladder storage for these models featured side stacking above the low side compartments. High side compartments for added storage were an option with center-stacked ladders.

Although the bulk of these units featured 100-foot aerials, the Ladder-Chief had an 85-foot option, and a three-section, 75-foot Water-Chief was available for mounting on a pumper. The 75-foot Water-Chief required only two A-style, hydraulic, rear outriggers with a 13-foot spread. Aerial ladder controls were at the pump panel and were also at the rear of the unit. The three-section, steel ladder used the same fly section as the taller models. This unit could be mounted on the Century, Pace-maker, Pioneer, or commercial chassis. Pumpers that were available for mounting the aerial included 1,000, 1,250, 1,500, 1,750, and 2,000 gallon-per-minute models with a 300-gallon water tank.

Boardman

In the early 1970s, the Boardman Company, located in Oklahoma, was in the metal fabrication business, and owned by Continental Boiler Works of St. Louis, Missouri. Boardman fabricated large pressure vessels for industry in addition to building between 50 and 70 fire trucks that were sold regionally for several years. In 1978, at a management meeting with the Continental Boiler managers, Boardman sales people mentioned that they could use a line of aerial devices to sell along with the pumpers. They were unable to attain an OEM agreement with Snorkel, which produced many of the popular aerial devices. Continental Boiler then purchased Reading Techmatic of Reading, Pennsylvania, a company building aerial devices, and began using the name Readi Tower along with the model numbers for the aerial products. The company offered a telescoping water tower with an aluminum rescue ladder, similar to Snorkel's Tele-Squrt, as a T50 with a 50-foot device or a T75 with a 75-foot device. The two-section T-50 used one set of A-style jacks at the rear with a spread of 11 feet, 11 inches. The three-section T-75 required two sets of A-jacks, with a spread of 13 feet, 3 inches for the forward set, and 10 feet, 4 inches at the rear. Also available was the A54, a 54-foot articulating water tower similar to the Squrt. Finally, the Boardman line had the TP, a telescoping platform (formerly the Teleboom). The platform was available as a 75-foot or 85-foot model. While the 75-foot was a midship design, the 85-foot had a midship- or rear-mounted option. The TPM-75SL was a 75-foot, midship-mounted platform. The TPM-85SL was a midship, 85-foot platform, and a TPR-85SL was the rear-mount. When Reading Techmatic produced the TP during the 1960s for Ward LaFrance, the top of the boom was fitted with a telescoping, aluminum rescue ladder. After Continental Boiler Works purchased the company, it changed the design, moving the

In 1980, E-ONE (then known as Emergency One, Inc.) was an OEM for the Fire Spire aerial by Hahn. The Hendrickson 1871-C low-profile chassis under this unit was one of the early aerial chassis available to apparatus builders that did not have their own proprietary chassis. When Robert Wormser, the founder of Emergency One, was unable to purchase exclusive rights to the Fire Spire aerial, he hired the ladder's original engineer to design an exclusive aerial out of aluminum for Emergency One.

ladder alongside the boom, lowering the travel height. When extended, the ladder had high handrails compared to the previous version, which was little more than a conventional ladder without separate handrails.

In a three-year period leading up to 1980, roughly 50 Readi-Tower units were sold, which did not prove to be enough volume to maintain the plant in Reading. The facility was closed and with it went the name Reading Techmatic. Boardman moved production to Oklahoma, renaming the aerial operation Readi Tower Corporation.

Emergency One

In 1974, events began to unfold that would ultimately alter the fire apparatus industry. An inventor in Florida named Robert Wormser decided to build an ambulance in his barn out of aluminum instead of steel, which was the standard. After selling the ambulance, he tried his hand at building a fire truck. As the story goes, he ventured into each project simply because he had never done either before. He started Emergency One in Ocala, Florida, where the company remains today, and offered fire apparatus bodies out of aluminum instead of the industry standard, which was galvaneal steel. In 1979, Emergency One needed to finance its growth; this was accomplished when Federal Signal Corporation bought the company. Within nine years, sales were close to $40 million.

In the early 1970s, and for many years after, the majority of fire apparatus manufacturers were aligned with one of the two major fire pump suppliers, Hale or Waterous. As discussed in detail under the Hahn subheading in this chapter, Hale wanted to provide an aerial product for customers that did not produce their own aerials. Emergency One, a Hale distributor, entered into the aerial products market in 1976 when National Foam, a sister company to Hale Pumps, released the Fire Spire aerial ladder. Emergency One was one of a small handful of companies that initially acquired an OEM contract with National Foam. The aerial program at Emergency One went under the model name of StratoSpear. The original release was a 106-foot, four-section, steel aerial, followed by the later release of an 85-foot model. The torque box was built of steel tubing and mounted above the chassis frame rails. Four A-style jacks were attached to the truss and provided support for aerial operations with a spread of 10 feet, 6 inches. The aerial featured "K" bracing on the ladder rungs and provided for the use of a waterway along the three base sections, a length of 85 feet, or as an added option to the tip. The waterway capacity was 1,000 gallons per minute with the ability to operate 90 degrees off the side of the ladder when mounted at the 85-foot level. This was one of the newer generation aerial ladder designs that was rated to work at any level of elevation or rotation while fully extended. The weight capacity at the tip was 200 pounds. By 1979, the StratoSpear aerial (Fire Spire) was also offered as an 85-foot aerial. Either length could be ordered on a single- or tandem-axle custom chassis from Duplex, Hendrickson, Pemfab, or Spartan. Available models were

This 100-foot Grove aerial ladder with serial number 721010 went to Cicero, Illinois, on a Ford C-Series commercial chassis in 1973. The American Fire Apparatus Company of Battle Creek, Michigan, sold the unit and fabricated the body. American was one of the primary OEM companies selling the Grove devices in the late 1960s and early 1970s. Shortly after this aerial was produced, Grove sold off the fire service aerial ladder division to concentrate exclusively on the production of cranes for the construction industry. This aerial, like many in the early 1970s carried a life net to catch people jumping from buildings. This practice was not commonly used and the life net was phased out in the ensuing years.

straight trucks or quints with water tanks and pumps. Emergency One also offered an extensive list of options for ground-ladder placement and body compartment designs.

In 1979, Emergency One offered to buy the Fire Spire design from Hahn, which had been producing the ladders since aquiring the design from National Foam in 1977. When an agreement could not be reached between the two companies, Robert Wormser, Emergency One's president, hired Bob Vanstone, the structural engineer who had designed the Fire Spire, to design an exclusive line of aluminum aerial devices for Emergency One.

Grove

In the early 1970s, Grove still concentrated on manufacturing cranes, farm implements, and rollback units for the towing industry, while maintaining a small section that produced aerials for the fire service in a corner of one building. In 1970, due to the efforts of the regional distributor, Texas cities were still the main customers for Grove aerials, although the Chicago Fire Department received five 100-foot ladders. A few units were shipped elsewhere through 1971, but it was not until 1972 that Grove aerials were consistently shipped to fire departments in many states.

In 1970, Grove was successful and wanted to sponsor an open house in a barn that it owned. The barn was in disrepair and badly in need of painting before the event. A painting contractor from Ephrata was contacted for the job. The painter used cherry picker–type trucks for painting and became intrigued by the Grove fire ladders that were at the plant. Viewing plant workers walking along the ladder at a zero-degree elevation, the painter pondered having the handrails raised and replacing the rubber rung covers with metal plates for his painting applications. The painter then discovered that this device could be placed at one corner of a barn and it could still reach two sides of the building. By using this method, a barn could be painted in one day by three men. He purchased one of these units and later purchased an 85-foot ladder tower. They were mounted on Mack R-model chassis and outfitted with an air compressor, mixing system, and storage for 55-gallon drums of paint. Grove's efforts to have its barn painted for the open house would have far reaching consequences—not only for Grove but for fire truck manufacturing and the fire service in general.

In 1972, Grove hired a new product manager to oversee the fire ladders division. He initiated some market research that included talking with OEMs and fire departments about concerns or desires for aerial apparatus. Comments that he received about straight ladders included three basic complaints. First, it could be awkward and tiresome climbing to the tip of the ladder, as opposed to using an aerial with a bucket that allowed firefighters to ride up and down. Second, it was cumbersome to drag a hose line and monitor nozzle up the ladder for master stream operations. The third concern, often repeated, was that the pipe at the end of the ladder could be moved only about 7 degrees to either side while flowing water. This required firefighters to make adjustments in the ladder position for greater reach at a fire scene. The major drawback that was brought up concerning the articulated or telescoping style platform aerials on the market was the lack of a means for mass evacuation. The number of people who could be rescued was limited because the platform had to be lowered to the ground prior to returning for the next group of people. This could be dangerous at a fire scene when occupants might panic seeing the bucket leave without them.

Grove engineers set out to develop a ladder that would be combined with a platform to transport firefighters to the upper floors or roof, and still enable mass evacuations without moving the aerial device. The unit also had to incorporate a telescopic pipe from the pump to the platform to simplify master stream operations, plus increase the working range of the monitor nozzle. During this time, Henning Anderson of American Fire Apparatus was waiting for Reading Techmatic to build an 85-foot, telescopic platform aerial that was on order. As the chassis sat at the facility in Reading for a prolonged period of time without any progress, Anderson approached Grove to be the first user of its new aerial design. With some engineering and design work, Grove introduced the 85-foot, rear-mounted ladder tower. The waterway issue became a basic cylinder design and the nozzle mounted at the tip was able to achieve 180 degrees of lateral sweep with a 3,000 gallon-per-minute maximum output. Grove used a telescoping aerial ladder with a platform mounted at the end to compete with the Snorkel. The company took the 100-foot ladder and removed the fly section. Grove also redesigned and modified the tapered base section to a full-width design all the way to the end. In the travel position, the platform rested above and slightly in front of the truck cab. Until 1972, when this product was introduced, all platform aerials were either articulating boom units or midship-mounted apparatus with the platform hanging over the rear of the truck. The midship units were telescopic in design with solid booms from

The midship aerial design was popular with fire departments that were concerned with vehicle travel height for bridges or older fire stations. The American Fire Apparatus Company built many apparatus with the fire pump controls and piping at the front of the cab. This unit was built in 1972 on a Duplex D300 custom fire truck chassis with a 100-foot, midship-mounted Grove 4S-100 aerial ladder that was built with a tapered front edge on the base section. The unit was delivered to North Aurora, Illinois, with a 750 gallon-per-minute pump capacity.

Baker and Reading Techmatic, or lattice-style box booms from Sutphen. In either case, where available, the ladders that provided egress to the platform were minimal when compared with a standard aerial ladder with high hand-rails. The new Grove ladder tower provided a conventional aerial ladder design in combination with a platform. After several revisions, the first three-section, 85-foot, Grove tower ladder was delivered in 1973 to the Pine Castle Fire Department in Florida. It had a 700-pound tip load with a pre-piped waterway, one monitor nozzle in the platform, and electricity to power accessories from the platform. This was known as a model 3S-85.

In an effort to keep up with the demands of the fire service, Grove wanted to upgrade the straight ladders to accommodate a pre-piped waterway. The existing ladder had to be beefed up to withstand the added load and force from the water. The 200-pound tip load New Generation aerial line was introduced as the NG 4S-100. This heavier ladder used a double chain on each side and dual orbit motors to drive extension, replacing the single-drive orbit motor and

single extension chain on prior Grove ladders. instead of the tapered appearance at the edge of the older ladder, the New Generation had squared ends with 90-degree angles like the ladder tower. When equipped with a pre-piped waterway, the monitor nozzle protruded unprotected past the bedded ladder sections. Stabilization was achieved with four H-style outriggers. Pierce was a Grove OEM, and the first pre-piped ladder went to Evansville, Indiana, with a Pierce body.

The New Generation ladder and the ladder tower shared the same basic ladder components. The NG 4S-100 was a 3S-85 with a fourth section added and no bucket. All of Grove's manufacturing was based on interchangeable components to adapt to other products. These new items introduced in 1974 became the basis for many future aerials.

Grove used model numbers that indicated the number of ladder sections followed by the material used to build the aerial, and then the length of the aerial. A 3S-65 was a three-section, steel ladder that could reach 65 feet. Prior to 1972 and the introduction of the New Generation Series, Grove offered the 3S-65, 3S-75, 4S-85, and the 4S-100 aerials, all with 200-pound tip loads. These ladders had a tapered front edge on the base section.

Grove aerials were marketed through OEM relationships with several fire apparatus builders between 1959 and 1972. These included American Fire Apparatus, Boardman, Bruco, Central, Darley, Hahn, FMC, Howe (later Grumman), Imperial, Oren, Pierce, Sanford, Seagrave, Towers, Universal, Van Pelt, and Ward LaFrance.

The crane business for Grove was growing so rapidly that by 1973 the company wanted to divest from the rollback, farming, and fire service divisions. Grove contacted the larger OEMs and tried, unsuccessfully, to sell the aerial ladder production to them. In 1974, the Grove fire ladder operations, along with parts and the current backlog of orders, were sold to a group of six investors that included employees, dealers, customers, and other outside individuals.

Hahn

Hahn had been an OEM selling Grove and Thibault ladders, but the history of the Hahn aerial products actually began at National Foam. Hale Pumps, the fire pump manufacturer, and National Foam were sister companies. Hale was interested in making an aerial device available to apparatus builders that used the Hale pumps but did not have an aerial program of their own. In 1975, National Foam designed the Fire Spire ladder. The company built roughly 10 units from 1975 through 1977. This was an all-steel, four-section, 106-foot aerial with a 200-pound tip load rating. The Fire Spire utilized four A-style jacks with a 10-foot spread, and was offered as a straight truck or a quint with a water tank and a Hale pump. The first Fire Spire was built on a Ward LaFrance Ambassador chassis with an ornate paint scheme to be displayed at the 1975 IAFC convention in Las Vegas. The Santa Rosa, California, fire department purchased this unit off the show floor without seeing the aerial perform. Several of the first units built by National Foam were marketed by Ward LaFrance and one went to Crown Firecoach. Two or three of the remaining units went to an upstart company that was new to the fire apparatus market and did not have an aerial product of its own. That company was Emergency One in Ocala, Florida.

In 1977, two years after National Foam introduced the Fire Spire aerial, Hahn Motors bought the design and took over marketing and production. Hahn would go on to build 61 Fire Spire aerial ladders. At this time, Emergency One, Fire Tec, and Grumman were OEM distributors of the Fire Spire. During its association with Hahn, Grumman sold 11 Fire Spire aerials, Fire Tec sold 6, and Emergency One sold 15. In 1979, the founder of Emergency One offered to buy the Fire Spire design from Hahn. When the two companies could not agree on terms for a sale, Emergency One withdrew from the negotiations. With the help of the original Fire Spire designer, Emergency One went on

to design and build aerial ladders with a similar truss system from aluminum instead of steel. Also in 1979, the first 85-foot Fire Spire was sold to Ft. Knox, Kentucky. Seven 85-foot Fire Spire aerials were eventually built.

In 1986, Hahn introduced a four-section, 75-foot Fire Spire with a 200-pound tip load. This smaller unit was built on a pumper chassis and utilized only two rear stabilizers. Nine of the aerials were produced with the first going to Linder New Jersey that same year. Only seven were completed by Hahn, the remaining two were acquired by KME at auction in 1992. After struggling for several years in the late 1980s, Hahn motors went out of business in December of 1989.

Hendrickson

In 1972, Hendrickson Mobile Equipment Company began to market custom fire truck chassis in conjunction with International Harvester. As the pioneer in non-proprietary custom chassis for the fire service, Hendrickson found buyers eager to acquire a chassis made specifically for their industry. Soon smaller manufacturers would have the ability to compete with the companies such as American LaFrance, Crown, Mack, Maxim, Pirsch, Seagrave, and

This unusual looking aerial device is a Morita-Lift from Japan. The Chicago Fire Department purchased one of these 135-foot aerials in 1974 to cover the high-rise buildings downtown. Bodywork was by Pierce and it was mounted on a Hendrickson 1871-S chassis without the crew seating area. The aerial featured an elevator that carried the crew up to the tip of the six-section ladder. The aerial design did not allow for a body with much compartment space. The ground ladder storage required quite a bit of room and limited the size of the cab.

Calavar tried to compete with the popular Snorkel articulating platform in the 1970s with 90-, 100-, 125-, and 150-foot aerials. They were able to achieve greater height than the Snorkel units because, in addition to the two articulating booms, Calavar units also had the capability to telescope for further distance. Hendrickson and Seagrave supplied the heavy-duty custom chassis for Calavar. This Firebird 90 on a Hendrickson 1871-S chassis was built in 1975 and was one of three Firebird units for the Sacramento, California, fire department. Calavar's main business was supplying the industrial sector with aerial devices. When the fire service market did not provide the business that the company had hoped for, Calavar returned to building the industrial units exclusively.

Ward LaFrance, which offered custom chassis of their own. The model 1871-S (named for the year of the great Chicago fire) featured Hendrickson's chassis and suspension expertise with a very modern, square, open canopy cab from Truck Cab Manufacturers (TCM).

In a matter of a few years, Hendrickson chassis were also being ordered for specialized aerial apparatus. Some of the first units were built to carry Firebird articulating aerials by Calavar. Another of the early Hendrickson units had a rather odd looking design with a short cab and no canopy area. This was a tandem-axle chassis that supported a 135-foot Japanese aerial device called a Morita-Lift. Bodywork was by Pierce and the unit went into service with the Chicago Fire Department. In the next year, Hendrickson chassis were used for Pitman Snorkels and telescoping aerial platforms by a new company called LTI that had acquired the production rights of Grove Manufacturing's fire service aerials. The LTI units were sold through OEMs and featured bodywork by American, Howe, Pierce, and others. Emergency One also used the low-profile 1871-S for the Simon Snorkels that it sold.

In 1976, the 1871-C was released, offering a contoured cab design for those who preferred this look to the flat, square 1871-S. During this time, Emergency One became a customer of Hendrickson through a marketing agreement with Hahn to sell the Fire Spire aerial. As Hendrickson continued to provide chassis for most of the fire apparatus builders, it worked closely with Emergency One during the design stages of the Emergency One aerial program. Engineers at Hendrickson, in conjunction with Emergency One engineers, designed the integral chassis torque box configuration that is still used on today's Emergency One aerials. When Emergency One announced its aerial program, the Hendrickson 1871-WS (the wider version of the flat 1871-S) was the initial custom chassis and cab that was offered with the 110-foot aluminum ladders. It was not until 1983 that any of the other custom chassis were available with the new Emergency One aerials.

In 1985, shortly after Hendrickson introduced a tilt-cab chassis to the fire service, Kovatch purchased the fire apparatus chassis division of Hendrickson Mobile Equipment, and the custom line of fire truck chassis was incorporated into KME Fire Apparatus. At the same time, the remaining assets, including the custom conventional trucks, were sold to HME, a newly formed company that would later enter the custom fire chassis business.

Imperial/Pemfab

In 1970, Pemberton Fabricators of Rancocas, New Jersey, entered the fire apparatus industry under the name of Imperial Fire Apparatus with the delivery of its first rig to the Good Will Fire Company Number 1 of Pemberton, New Jersey. The company produced pumpers, chassis, and fabricated aerial bodies but were not able to sustain operations

One of the three independent custom fire truck chassis companies in the mid-1970s was marketed under the name of Pemfab. Pemfab competed with Duplex and Hendrickson. In 1975, Pierce was an OEM with a new aerial ladder company called LTI and sold this 85-foot, 3S-85 ladder tower with a Pemfab chassis to the fire department in Bensenville, Illinois. The black label on the ladder near the platform carries the early LTI logo design.

due to a lack of sales. Approximately 200 units were built in the three years between 1970 and 1973 with aerials accounting for less than 10 percent. In 1973, with new personnel, it emerged as Chassis by Pemfab and produced a line of custom fire truck chassis available to any apparatus builder in the fire service. Using TCM contour cabs, plus a unique TCM exclusive design called the Wedge, Chassis by Pemfab were purchased for aerials by several OEMs. Another management change resulted in the company's re-emergence as Pemfab Trucks in 1983 with an expanded line of fire chassis. In the early years of E-ONE's aerial program and before the launch of the E-ONE Hurricane custom chassis in 1984, the Florida builder was a big user of Pemfab chassis, purchasing almost 150 of them over 10 years.

In 1986, the product line grew even larger and Pemfab Trucks listed 52 OEMs poised to purchase chassis, although only about 18 of these were in the aerial market. American LaFrance contracted with Pemfab for over 100 chassis between 1986 and 1992, for the Century and Pacemaker Series units. The majority of these chassis were used for pumpers. Pemfab Trucks stopped production in 1996 and a small fire apparatus company called Fire Cab, a division of Chambersburg Engineering, purchased the remaining assets.

Ladder Towers, Inc.

In 1973, Grove Manufacturing decided to divest itself of all divisions other than crane building for the construction market. Farm implements, rollback trucks, and aerial devices for the fire service were all sold off during that year to separate buyers. The fire service product line was purchased by a group of six investors in 1974. Original plans called for the company to locate in Berkeley Springs, West Virginia, but instead it opened in the Conestoga Industrial Park in Leola, Pennsylvania. The new company was named Ladder Towers, Incorporated (LTI), reflecting the premier product that it had to offer. One of the investors, Mahlon Zimmerman, who became chairman of the board, was the barn painter mentioned in the section about Grove.

When LTI began operations in June 1974, it had several finished ladder sections from the Grove facility that needed to be assembled and painted to produce new aerials. LTI also emerged with the Grove backlog of customer orders that needed to be produced and shipped under the LTI name. The first completed ladder out of the new facility, serial number 732480, was a 4S-85 mid-mount aerial that was shipped to Fort Thomas, Kentucky, in July of that year

The first Challenger aerial with serial number 761413 was sold to the fire department in New Lenox, Illinois. It was built on a Pemfab chassis with the proprietary Wedge cab design. The cab was made exclusively for Pemfab by TCM. The large LTI sign on the ladder represented the new corporate design for the company. The Challenger was a lighter weight ladder than the New Generation Series, which enabled this unit to be built on a single rear-axle chassis.

with a body by Howe. This unit was completed in a new building that did not yet have a roof, a floor, or doors. The completed aerial, ready for paint, was parked in a short bay with the aerial ladder extended out of the building. A 40-foot truck trailer was backed up, allowing the ladder to extend inside the trailer. This structure became the paint booth for the first LTI aerial ladder. Grove ladders were painted silver or grey until they began using white in the early 1970s. LTI painted their ladders white. The silver was hard to clean and the white offered better visibility for the fire department at night or in smoke.

The LTI product line included the 85-foot, three-section, steel ladder tower and the four-section, 100-foot, New Generation ladder. The line also offered three- and four-section aerial ladders with 65-, 75-, 85-, and 100-foot lengths of the tapered Grove design. The New Generation became the primary product and the original Grove design began to fade away. The 3S-85 ladder tower was refined at LTI to allow for more efficient manufacturing than the prototype designs from Grove would allow. Grove had built

seven tower ladders, including Pine Castle, Florida, Eau Claire, Wisconsin, Elkins Park, Pennsylvannia, Oakland Park, Florida, St. Petersburg, Florida, Fairfax City, Virginia, and one for the barn painting business. Subsequent ladder towers were built in Leola.

During 1974 and 1975, there was a chassis shortage for LTI, and completed aerials with torque boxes and outriggers were stacking up waiting to be mounted. This was a tough time financially for LTI since payment for completed ladders was not coming in. As production increased, LTI was completing up to five units per month in the early part of 1975. Ladders were sold through OEMs that were not used to this much volume (during the Grove days ladders came out only every six weeks). OEMs could not build bodies fast enough so LTI started building bodies in 1976 and competing with the OEMs to keep cash flowing. Most units were mounted onto Oshkosh A-Series chassis with 84-inch TCM contour cabs. Some of the bodies were subcontracted to companies like Hahn and Hammerly, but were delivered with an LTI nameplate. The first unit with an LTI body, an NG 4S-100, went to Topeka, Kansas, in 1976.

The product line included the 4S-100 Series. This was a four-section, steel, 100-foot aerial ladder that could be configured as a rear-mount, mid-mount, or TDA. There were two versions of this ladder. The New Generation ladder had an optional waterway, a 200-pound tip load, breathing air to the tip, and tip controls. The rear-mount and the mid-mount both used four H-style, out and down outriggers, while the tractor-drawn used two swing-out stabilizers of the same style. When the New Generation aerial was introduced, the nozzle for a pre-piped waterway protruded past the tip of the fly section. To accommodate this, the fly section was extended past the nozzle in 1976, making the aerial length 104 feet and the model name NG 4S-104. The end of the extended fly section had a squared-off design. These aerials were also available with a tapered design or with custom-length fly sections, adjusting the overall length of the vehicle as required by the fire department.

LTI needed a lighter weight, more competitively priced ladder to challenge the marketplace. The company reintroduced the original Grove ladder, with minor updates, as the Challenger Series. This was the second version of the 4S-100, now called the 4S-100C. This 100-foot ladder was also available in the three configurations (rear-mounted, mid-mounted, and tractor-drawn) with a 200-pound tip load, but was not offered with a waterway. The only amenities it came with were an intercom and spotlights at the tip. It was made with high-strength Corten steel that was commonly used in bridge construction. This steel could be left un-painted on bridges. The outward appearance of the Challenger ladder was easily identified by the upward tapering of the end of the base section. It went from 15 inches to 6 inches in width. Very few tractor-drawn Challenger Series aerials were produced. The first Challenger Series rear-mount aerial, serial number 761413, went to the fire department in New Lenox, Illinois, with a Pemfab Wedge cab and an LTI body. One advantage of the Challenger aerial over the New Generation was its weight. The Challenger was lighter than the New Generation and could be installed onto either a single rear axle chassis or a tandem-axle chassis.

The New Generation Series also had a four-section, 85-foot, steel ladder that was offered as a rear-mount, mid-mount, and TDA—although no tractor-drawn units were ever built.

LTI also offered a 65-foot and 75-foot ladder. The 3S-65 and the 3S-75 were both three-section steel ladders with 200-pound tip load ratings. They were available in rear-mount and mid-mount configurations with optional waterways. Few of these units were actually built. In a move that was years ahead of its time, the Young Fire Equipment Company, an OEM, produced the Fire Commander Series in the mid-1970s and utilized the 3S-65 New Generation ladder mounted on a tandem rear axle chassis. The unit was marketed as an attack-capable aerial. The first unit, serial number 750763, was built on a tilt-cab Ford chassis for

Hillsboro, New Jersey. The Fire Commander had a pump and 300-gallon water tank, but had minimal room for ground ladders. LTI wanted to offer a 75-foot ladder for this product, but the New Generation 3S-75 was too heavy for a unit with a pump and water tank. LTI began to work on developing a new, lightweight, 75-foot aerial ladder.

In 1978, LTI moved the service facilities and the body company, Conestoga Custom Products, from Leola to Ephrata, Pennsylvania.

Also in 1978, LTI incorporated Conestoga Custom Products to fabricate bodies and complete aerials, both as a means of helping to keep up with the demand by the OEMs and to act as an independent distributor. LTI had production capability in excess of the number of units that were being sold by the OEMs. Many early units were sold with name-plates corresponding to the OEM but with bodies by Conestoga since the OEMs did not have the capacity to handle all of the fabrication themselves. Most of the units that were shipped with Conestoga labels were produced for fire departments in New York, New Jersey, and Pennsylvania.

LTI built a one-of-a-kind aerial in 1979. It was a three-section, 75-foot, rear-mounted ladder tower on an Oshkosh L-Series low-profile chassis for the Friendship Fire Company #1, of Danville, Pennsylvania. This unit was designed to accommodate height and length restrictions in the firehouse using an NG 3S-75 base and midsection with an extended fly section. The unit carried serial number 790471.

In 1979, LTI introduced the three-section, 100-foot ladder tower. The first unit, called an MT-100, went to Glendale, Colorado, on an Oshkosh A-Series chassis with a Pierce body. It had a two-door TCM contour cab and offered a 700-pound tip load. The MT-100 utilized four H-style outriggers with a 16-foot jack spread, but there were limits on the horizontal reach below 45 degrees. The 85-foot tower was also still available. Up until that time, LTI aerials used a dual roller chain system for ladder extension and retraction. This was replaced by a hydraulic cylinder system when the 100-foot tower was introduced. Product upgrades for the 85-foot tower and the New Generation ladders were made to include the new hydraulic system. These upgraded products became the H Series. The 85-foot tower was the HT-85 and the New Generation 4S-100 became the HL4S-100, with the "H" designating hydraulic extension.

The Challenger Series was not upgraded and remained available only for a short time afterwards, ending in 1981. The cylinder extension modifications to the 85-foot tower ladder meant that the base section closest to the turntable

The Aerialscope achieved popularity and recognition through an association with the FDNY, becoming a staple of the FDNY fleet. The Aerialscopes had a 75-foot, midship-mounted, telescoping aerial platform with a built-in waterway. They were built on single-axle, CF-600 Series Mack chassis. Roughly 350 of the 75-foot Aerialscope towers were produced for Mack between 1970 and 1990, with the majority sold to the FDNY.

a mid-mount, telescoping aerial platform with a built-in waterway. It was available with a length extendable to 75 feet. It used six stabilizers, three on each side. Two downriggers were located on either side of the cab front, two downriggers were at the rear tailboard, and two hydraulic, A-style radial stabilizers were positioned by the center-mounted turntable. Aerialscopes were built on a single-axle CF-600 Series Mack chassis. The telescoping platform had a weight rating of 1,000 pounds in the basket. The pre-piped, telescoping waterway was quick to put into service. The aerial controls were located at the turntable as well as in the bucket by means of a joystick. The platform offered 18 square feet of space, and the body provided for 163 feet of ground ladders, accessible from the rear.

The line was expanded in 1974 to include a tandem-axle unit, in addition to a tandem-axle unit with a midship-mounted or booster pump. Bodies were built by Mack and offered in a standard configuration. The advantages of ordering a unit with a tandem rear axle were improved braking, the ability to accommodate larger engines, and the option of added storage space to carry more equipment. The single-axle models were built with 28,000-pound rear axles, while the tandem-axle models were increased to 48,000 pounds. When the tandem axle was introduced, Mack also redesigned the steering components for a better cramp angle, allowing for a tighter turning radius. The FDNY began to augment its fleet of single-axle Aerialscopes with tandem-axle models when they became available. FDNY began to realize a trade-off between the ability to carry additional equipment with the tandem-axle models, and the longer overall vehicles that became increasingly difficult to maneuver in some areas. Just fewer than 350 75-foot Aerialscope towers were produced for Mack between 1970 and 1990.

The Mack CF chassis was also a popular choice for fire departments that purchased aerial products by Snorkel. Beginning in 1968, almost 200 Snorkel products were mounted on CF chassis with bodywork from several OEMs, though the vast majority had Pierce bodies. These included 55-foot, 65-foot, 75-foot, and 85-foot Snorkels along with 50-foot and 75-foot Tele-Squrts.

needed strengthening to stiffen the back end. This change was necessary because of the added weight and force generated by the cylinders. Steel plates were added between the base rail and the upper handrail to enclose the open sides of the base section. The 100-foot tower ladder never needed these plates since that product had been designed with the new extension system from the ground up.

Mack

One of the most recognizable and longest running names in fire apparatus made its own aerials for only a short period of time. From as early as 1929, Mack marketed aerials as part of its product line, but began relying on those made by a third party in the late 1940s. From that point on, Mack produced chassis, cabs, powerplants, and bodies. Many aerials were marketed as Mack products. Whether it was a desire to own a Mack because it was the best or because it would match other apparatus in a fleet, some fire departments simply wanted a Mack chassis under an aerial device that was produced by someone else. The Mack chassis was found under many aerials by Pirsch, Snorkel, and LTI in addition to those marketed through Mack.

As mentioned in the previous chapter, Mack utilized Maxim aerial ladders beginning in the late 1940s. The Maxim ladders were not exclusively available through Mack; they could be purchased through Ward LaFrance and also directly from Maxim.

The Aerialscope, probably the most recognizable aerial device sold by Mack, was introduced in 1964. It was made particularly famous because of its association with the largest fire department in the world, the FDNY. The Aerialscope was

Maxim

In 1970, an engineer named Bob Vanstone designed and developed a four-section, 100-foot aerial ladder for Maxim. Had it been built, this would have been the first

Maxim aerial ladders were used by several OEM companies in addition to being mounted on apparatus built by Maxim. This four-section, 100-foot, midship aerial ladder was mounted on a Maxim Marauder chassis in 1974 for Westchester, Illinois. The unit has no pump or water tank. Mounted at the rear of the unit, above the low compartments, is a nozzle that would be placed at the tip of the aerial for elevated master stream operations. The hose to supply the nozzle sits in a trough along the side of the ladder and would be dragged along the ladder by hand.

500-pound, "K"-braced aerial ladder in the fire service. The tip rating represented a fully extended aerial at a zero-degree elevation. The "K" bracing, which is used in most ladders built from that point to the current day, gives the ladder lateral stiffness. The Maxim management team refused to put this new aerial ladder into production at that time. The ladder was eventually built in the late 1970s and was marketed through Ward LaFrance.

In 1972, Maxim introduced 85-foot and 100-foot rear-mount options for its light-duty aerials. Maxim also introduced a four-section, 75-foot mid-mount, which was in essence a shortened version of the 85-foot ladder. Maxim was still selling aerials to Crown in addition to building the complete unit themselves.

In 1976, a company called North Street Associates purchased Maxim and Ward LaFrance. In 1977, the decision was made to implement the 500-pound heavy-duty ladder that was designed for Maxim in 1970. Three or four of these expensive units were built, one of which was modified with two fly sections and sold as a 50-foot water tower. The company filed for bankruptcy in 1978, but continued operating. One of Maxim's long-time dealers bought the assets and re-opened the company in 1981. The Maxim Motor Company then operated for three to four years selling pumpers and aerials before closing down again.

Pierce

Pierce Manufacturing, previously Pierce Auto Body Works, Inc., was fabricating utility bodies and fire pumper bodies, in addition to being the prime subcontractor building Snorkel bodies in the early 1970s. As a means of entering the aerial fire truck market in 1972, Pierce began to market a 35-foot and a 45-foot, two-section, telescoping ladder with a section at the end where a person could stand. The Aerial-ETT, as it was called, was a device used by utility companies. During the 1970s, Pierce sold 12 of these units, split evenly between the two sizes. The first unit went to Ventor City, New Jersey, and the second was sold overseas to Columbia. The Aerial-ETT did not prove popular and was not offered for long.

In 1973, Pierce was looking to build a national dealer network to sell pumpers, and it wanted to offer an aerial device. At the time, Pierce was still the prime subcontractor for Snorkel devices, but it was not involved with the sales. Much to Snorkel's disappointment, Pierce contracted to buy a telescoping water tower and rescue ladder device made by the Highway Trailer Company in Wisconsin, as part of a larger order of units

The Aerial-ETT was a ladder device used by utility companies that was adapted by Pierce for use in the fire service. It was offered in 35-foot and 45-foot lengths, but only 12 units were sold to fire departments.

The Crown Firecoach Company in Los Angeles built apparatus for many fire departments throughout California as well as other states. The company was also an OEM for Snorkel. This 1978 unit for El Segundo featured bodywork by Pierce with the trademark black vinyl-covered operator's panel. The 75-foot Tele-Squrt used four A-style jacks and a tandem rear axle chassis.

several years but did not have exclusivity with any of the products. The full LTI line was available to fire departments through several different OEMs. The first LTI that Pierce sold was delivered to the Wayne Township Fire Department outside of Indianapolis in 1974.

In 1979, Pierce introduced the Pierce Arrow custom fire chassis and offered it for aerials shortly thereafter. The company released other new chassis that also were available for aerials, including the Dash in 1983 and the Lance in 1985.

Pirsch

Pirsch had a long history in the fire apparatus industry, especially with aerial ladders. The Pirsch all-aluminum junior and senior aerials were in service throughout the country. Pirsch offered midship-mounted units, rear-mounts, and TDAs. The mid-mounts and the rear-mounts were available as straight ladder trucks or as quints with a pump and water tank. A junior aerial was one of the shorter, 65-foot models, while the longer 75-foot, 85-foot, and 100-foot styles were called senior aerials. These ladders featured all-riveted construction with

for Syracuse, New York. The unit very closely resembled Snorkel's Tele-Squrt. Eight of these devices, named High Stream, were shipped on Hendrickson chassis. Syracuse received seven Tele-Squrts with Pierce bodywork at the same time. The Tele-Squrts were purchased through Snorkel. These were the only High Stream units that Pierce ever sold.

In 1974, Pierce became an OEM to sell LTI aerial devices. Pierce sold platform aerials and straight ladders for

Snorkel products were purchased mainly through Snorkel, who would then purchase the chassis and body to complete the unit. Pierce was the prime subcontractor for bodywork to Snorkel, even in some cases where a proprietary chassis was required. This was the case with this Pirsch Safety Cab for Champaign, Illinois, which was ordered with a 54-foot Squrt articulating water tower in 1970.

The Lisle-Woodridge Fire Protection District in Illinois was a loyal Pirsch customer and requested this one-of-a-kind aerial in 1979 to match its fleet. This was the only LTI to be mounted on the Pirsch Safety Cab chassis. Along the ladder is a hose chute to simplify deployment of supply hose for the pre-piped waterway. Pirsch did the bodywork and the tower length was 85 feet.

200-pound capacities, although this was not a rating for the tip. They had a "T" rail design that consisted of solid bottom rails with U-shaped upright support rails. A drum winch pulling the cables accomplished ladder extension. Due to the weight restraints, a pre-piped waterway was only available along the base section. The riveted design was instituted after George Layden, Pirsch's chief engineer in the 1930s, examined the riveted construction of the U.S. Steel building in Pittsburgh. He noted that the building was built to be flexible and carried this design into the ladders so that they would be flexible and not break. Pirsch enjoyed an excellent safety record regarding its ladders.

Pirsch built its own custom cabs and chassis, but also offered its aerials on commercial as well as custom fire truck chassis built by others. Pirsch's handmade cab was called the Safety Cab. Hendrickson, Spartan, Pemfab, and Mack chassis all sported Pirsch aerials, although the Mack chassis was particularly popular. One Pirsch chassis was made available for a different type of aerial device when the Lisle-Woodridge Fire Protection District in Illinois wanted a ladder tower to match its fleet of Pirsch Safety Cabs. Pirsch, who did not produce its own platform aerial, accommodated the customer request with a one-of-a-kind, 85-foot, LTI ladder tower that allowed the fire department to have a matching

fleet. The aerial device was shipped from LTI to Pirsch, where it was mounted on the Pirsch chassis, prior to having the body built around it. Pirsch was one of the original OEM builders in alliance with Snorkel and sold many Snorkel units of varying sizes built on Pirsch and Mack CF chassis with Pirsch bodywork.

The Safety Cab was hammered out by hand over a big iron frame by a single German craftsman in the Pirsch manufacturing facility in Kenosha, Wisconsin. When it became too cost prohibitive to continue producing the trademark cab-forward design, Pirsch began offering Cincinnati Cabs from TCM. Pirsch trimmed out these cabs with its own styling to distinguish them from the competition, then marketed them as Pirsch customs. Pirsch began to offer the TCM cabs in the late 1970s as a lower cost alternative to its own cabs, and then offered them exclusively after the last handmade custom cab was sold in 1981. Pirsch used the industry standard 86-inch-wide cabs followed by the 94-inch super wide cabs in 1983.

Body styles and compartmentation were uniquely customized and different from truck to truck. The manufacturing facility for Pirsch was a large building with three interior areas for production. The rear area was where the chassis were assembled. Then the unit would be rolled into the middle section and parked in a diagonal slot on one side of the building where it would remain for the balance of the manufacturing process. A team of craftsmen would begin hanging brackets and measuring sheet metal piece by piece to assemble the body on the chassis according to the design drawings. Upon completing the body, the unit would be rolled into the front area for painting and finishing of the cab and body.

The available ladders were all built with four sections and stabilization was achieved with four manual jacks or two hydraulic A-jacks. The manual jacks, standard on aerials for many years, were a screw-type jack system. This was a gravity fed system that required the operator to swing the jack out from the truck by hand. Then, after pulling a pin, the jack would corkscrew down from its own weight and would stop when it hit the ground. The pin was then replaced to lock the jack into place. Upon completion, the jack was cranked up by hand before being swung back into a compartment. The hydraulic jacks were a radial "A" configuration for mid-ship and rear-mounted aerials, and were stored in the up position along the side of the truck with the ground pads at the top. The jacks would fold down into place when needed. By the late 1970s, the hydraulic jacks had become standard on all Pirsch aerials. Tractor-drawn aerials used convertional A-style jacks.

All Pirsch quints were built with Hale pumps. In rare cases a fire department would require a Waterous pump and still want to purchase an aerial from Pirsch. These aerials were mounted on Mack CF chassis that were purchased with the pump already mounted. Truck bodies were built from galvaneal steel until the early 1980s, when aluminum was added as an option, but aluminum proved to be a more difficult material to build with when using the handmade methods employed at Pirsch.

Seagrave

Seagrave chassis were used for non-Seagrave aerial devices beginning in the late 1960s. Calavar Firebird articulating platform aerials, Snorkels, and the occasional LTI ladder tower were built on Seagrave custom chassis. Seagrave provided one of only a few of the chassis suitable to carry the enormous Calavar Firebird. Seagrave had an OEM alliance with Snorkel dating back to the 1960s. Snorkel mounted the aerial device on the Seagrave chassis and then either Seagrave or Pierce built the bodywork. The Rear Admiral was the standard Seagrave aerial ladder through the 1970s. Seagrave stopped building midship aerials in the early 1970s.

Snorkel

In the early 1970s, Snorkel Fire Equipment became Snorkel. Snorkel was purchased in 1971 by ATO, which also owned American LaFrance and Scott Aviation, the maker of self-contained breathing apparatus. After ATO acquired Snorkel, American LaFrance discontinued the Aero-Chief and Snorkels became available on American LaFrance chassis. Although the original intent of the purchase was to bolster American LaFrance, the market still wanted the Snorkel product line from other builders. In the following years, ATO needed a new identity and a name change and became Figgie International.

For the fire service, Snorkel was a builder of aerial devices only. Snorkel had to mount its products on a chassis and then add a truck body built elsewhere. The first units had steel baskets, which were replaced by aluminum in the early 1970s. This was a significant reduction in weight and allowed Snorkel to increase the payload of the units by 200 pounds. This meant that the 85-foot Snorkel could carry 900 pounds, up from 700 pounds with the steel basket.

Snorkel products were available to any fire department in one of two ways. Crown Coach, General Safety Equipment Corporation, Maxim Motors, Peter

The majority of Seagrave aerial ladder sections were painted silver, although the Liberty Fire Company Number 1 of Middletown, Pennsylvania, requested white for its 1978 unit. The space above the compartments was ideal for additional storage, in this case for supplemental scene lighting equipment. This unit had a flip-down seat added, facing forward outside of the canopy area.

Charlotte, Michigan, is the hometown of Spartan Motors. It was only natural that Charlotte's fire department would spec a Spartan chassis for its new 75-foot Snorkel in 1978. The Maxi-Vision style cab was popular with departments that wanted a larger windshield than what was offered with the conventional Cincinnati cab.

Pirsch Company, and Young Fire Equipment Company were able to purchase the aerial device from Snorkel and handle the complete sale. Otherwise, Snorkel was the prime contractor, dealing directly with the fire department. Snorkel would purchase the chassis, mount the aerial device, and then contract with Pierce Manufacturing for the body. Early Snorkels were commonly built on commercial Ford or International chassis, or custom chassis by FWD, Crown, Seagrave, International, Mack, Maxim, Oshkosh, or Pirsch.

In 1970, Snorkel replaced the original 50-foot device with a 55-foot unit. In the same year, Snorkel introduced a new product called the Tele-Squrt. This combined a 50-foot, lightweight rescue ladder with a remote controlled water tower. This model TS-50, two-section, telescopic aerial device was designed to mount on a conventional pumper, either as new equipment or as a retrofit to a pumper already in service. The ladder had a 400- to 800-pound weight rating, depending on the angle of elevation. One set of A-frame stabilizers mounted at the rear of the unit provided stabilization with a spread of 10 feet, 8 inches. The tip rating while flowing water was reduced to a 300-pound capacity at angles above 45 degrees.

In 1972, a 75-foot Tele-Squrt, model TS-75, was added to the product line. This was a three-section device with the same 300-pound tip load as the TS-50 while flowing water, and was available with an optional wireless remote control. As a rescue ladder, the tip rating ranged from 250 to 800 pounds, depending on the angle of elevation. Two sets of A-frame stabilizers were used with a spread of 11 feet at the rear and 15 feet, 3 inches for the front. The TS-75 could be mounted on a single-axle chassis, but tandem-axle chassis were most popular.

The Snorkel articulating platform aerial was offered in 55-, 65-, 75-, and 85-foot working heights. The articulated design allowed the platform to be positioned over a roof top, parapet wall, or other obstacles that would inhibit the straight path of a telescoping aerial. The Snorkel used A-frame stabilizers with a spread of 15 feet, 3 inches for the larger units. The 55'SFF had a 700-pound dry capacity, a 500-pound wet rating, and was mounted to a single-axle pumper. The 65'SFF had a 1,200-pound dry capacity, a 700-pound wet rating, and was also mounted on a single-axle chassis. The 75'SFF was rated at 1,050 pounds dry and 500 pounds wet, and the 85'SFF was rated at 900 pounds dry and 500 pounds wet. The 75'SFF could be ordered with a single- or tandem-axle chassis but the 85'SFF required a tandem-axle chassis.

In 1976, Snorkel introduced the Tele-Squrt 35. This was a small, two-section, telescopic boom that was designed as a retrofit to be mounted by a fire department onto existing pumpers. The unit did not require stabilizers and was purchased only by the U.S. Navy. Municipal fire departments wanted the 50-foot Tele-Squrt, which offered a stronger ladder. The Tele-Squrt 35 was discontinued within a short time period.

In 1977, Snorkel developed the Snorkel-Lift line of self-propelled work platforms for the construction trade. This segment of the company began to grow and eventually surpassed fire equipment sales.

In 1979, Snorkel stopped serving as the prime contractor for its units. This meant that all OEMs now dealt directly with the fire departments that were purchasing the vehicle, and the aerial devices were ordered from Snorkel.

Spartan

In 1975, Spartan Motors of Charlotte, Michigan, began to market custom fire truck chassis. The first chassis that it produced for the fire service was a model CF1000, which had shop order number 001, received a body by FMC, and was delivered to Covington, Ohio. The first chassis for an aerial product is believed to be shop order number 046, a model CFV3000. This was a tandem-axle chassis with a 92-inch-wide Maxi-Vision cab that was delivered in 1978 to the fire department in Charlotte, Michigan, Spartan's hometown. The unit had bodywork by Pierce and a 75-foot Snorkel articulating platform aerial.

Spartan went on to produce chassis for most of the fire apparatus builders with the exception, of course, of the companies that used their own chassis exclusively. In the early days, each Spartan chassis had a factory tag that was located on the firewall and contained a descriptive code. The letter designation at the beginning always represented the cab, while the numerical portion described the total number of axles and number of drive axles. For example, the third letter in a CFC2000 code followed by the number "2" meant that a contour cab was built with two axles. The cab could have been the original 86-inch width or the wider

94-inch model that replaced it. The "V" in CFV2000 signified an 86-inch-wide contoured Maxi-Vision cab on a two-axle chassis. An "H" in the code later represented the wider, 92-inch Maxi-Vision cab style, and a "G" described the flat 94-inch cab. As the codes grew, the numerical sequence described the number of axles first, followed by the position of the engine. The third letter signified how many wheels, and the fourth indicated the number of driving wheels. For example, a CFC-3064 had a contour cab, three axles with the engine located behind the front axle, and six wheels, four of which were drive wheels. A full in-depth analysis of the yearly progression of Spartan chassis options and cab configurations and a guide to the various codes can be found in *Pumpers: Workhorse Fire Engines*, mentioned in the introduction.

In 1983, Spartan introduced the Gladiator Series, an engine-forward design that positioned the engine between the driver and officer, allowing for a full-width cab in the rear crew area. Unlike competitors who were offering tilt-cab designs, Spartan designed a rollout assembly that permitted major service to be performed by sliding the engine out through the front grill opening. As with most new chassis, initial products were used for pumpers and rescues before being used for aerials. After several years of production, the Gladiator was re-introduced as a tilt-cab to better conform with industry expectations and requests from fire departments.

Sutphen

Sutphen was using the Cincinnati Cabs with chassis by International and Warner Swassey, although a customer could specify a commercial cab and chassis for their tower. Sutphen began to offer its own chassis beginning in 1972, and the first unit was an 85-foot tower with a diesel engine that went to the District of Columbia Fire Department.

The Sutphen tower offered an easy way for firefighters to enter the basket before it was moved from the stored position, saving critical time at a fire scene. In addition, each Sutphen tower was equipped with dual turrets. To maintain the midship-mounted units' low travel height, ground ladders were stacked on the sides of the vehicle, horizontally above the low side compartments. Sutphen offered a 300-gallon water tank and a 1,250 or 1,500 gallon-per-minute midship-mounted pump, making these units quints. Support was achieved with four stabilizers. Two H-style outriggers were placed midship, and two downriggers were located behind the rear axles. The center outriggers carried the entire load, while the rear supports were

The Harry Howard Hook and Ladder Company Number 1 of Port Chester, New York, was the home for this 1970 Sutphen 100 + aerial platform. Many fire companies on the east coast have their own names aside from the town, city, or borough where they work. These names were derived when the fire companies were organized in the 1800s or early 1900s.

designed to take the weight off of the springs. The top of the box frame aerial provided a means of getting to the platform and was aided by chrome grab rails that were mounted along the edges. This design did not prove to be a viable means of egress for some departments, and in the late 1970s Sutphen offered a version of its tower with a high handrail that still kept the waterway and cable away from the firefighters' feet during the climb.

Sutphen had competition from Baker and Ward LaFrance with midship-mounted, telescoping aerial platforms, though during the early 1970s Sutphen offered the longest reach. Sutphen also was the only builder that had an enclosed area that provided protection for the telescoping waterway.

The 85-foot design used winches and cables for ladder extension. This design was replaced with hydraulic cylinders in 1973 when the next generation tower was introduced. Two large, 5-inch cylinders were used at the midship turntable, which utilized big rams instead of the sheaves with smaller 1 1/2-inch cylinders. Sutphen offered a new model in addition to the 85-foot tower. The new unit was actually a 90-foot aerial measured at 70 degrees to the bottom of the platform. These units were produced with markings at the turntable labeling them with lengths of 100 + feet. Sutphen felt that the industry standard for measurement of ladder lengths at 90 degrees was misleading since the aerial could not be used at that angle in a practical manner. Sutphen used 75 degrees with full extension as a practical angle for working situations. Since the length measurement was to the tip of the ladder and did not account for the platform or a person standing and working in the platform, Sutphen 90-foot towers were deemed 100 + feet of practical working length with 1,000 pounds of payload in the platform and the ability to flow water at any angle. Although the majority of the Sutphen towers were sold in the Midwest areas surrounding the factory in Ohio, they were also finding their way to both coasts with over 500 going into the northeast.

In 1972, Sutphen installed a gas turbine engine that offered 500 horsepower with 1,800 pounds of torque in an aerial tower. The unit was sold to Boardman, Ohio, but the engine was pulled after delivery when Ford, the engine's producer, decided that the engines would not go into production because fuel economy was only 4 miles to the gallon. Other aerials that were in production at the time had the turbines replaced with 12-cylinder diesel engines.

Ward LaFrance was an early OEM representing Grove aerial ladders. Most were built with the unique P-80 Series cab, later renamed the Ambassador. In 1971, this unit was built with a 100-foot, rear-mounted Grove ladder and went to Streamwood, Illinois. Grove was painting their ladder grey unless white was specified by the OEM. In the early days, the OEM had to supply the white paint for the ladder.

Ward LaFrance

Prior to the 1970s, Ward LaFrance had an OEM alliance with Maxim and Grove to market aerial ladders. Ward LaFrance began looking for an aerial device that would be exclusive to them. In the early 1970s, they found a company in Reading, Pennsylvania, called Reading Techmatic, that had designed an aerial platform for the fire industry. Reading Techmatic's background consisted of making a 50-foot articulating boom with a de-icing system for the U.S. Air Force. In the late 1960s and the early 1970s, it produced over 100 of these booms. Reading Techmatic also made digger derricks for the construction and municipal markets.

In 1972, Ward LaFrance renamed the P-80 custom cab-forward chassis series the Ambassador. During the same year, they entered into an exclusive marketing agreement with Reading Techmatic to develop an articulating, 54-foot water tower as well as a telescoping water tower of the same length. Another product on the table was a telescoping elevating platform. Reading Techmatic agreed to design these products for Ward LaFrance to emulate the Snorkel product line, which featured an articulating water tower boom, a telescopic water tower, and an articulating platform aerial.

Later that same year, Reading introduced the Tele-boom, a 75-foot, midship-mounted, telescoping platform aerial that was similar in appearance to the Aerialscope. As a matter of fact, the engineers had fashioned the Teleboom after the Aerialscope, though the units differed in boom design. The Teleboom had a trapezoidal shape and only the base section was steel, while the other three sections were aluminum. The first Teleboom was built on a Ford CT900 tandem-axle chassis and purchased by the fire department in Fox Lake, Illinois. The second and only other Teleboom built for Ward LaFrance went to Louisville, Ohio, also on a Ford chassis. The Telebooms used one set of A-style jacks at the rear, one set of H-style outriggers behind the cab, and a scissors jack under the front bumper.

A midship, 85-foot Teleboom was also released with three units going to the United States Air Force on Duplex chassis and one other unit to Brookfield Township, Ohio, on a Ward LaFrance Ambassador chassis in 1978 with a pump and water tank. One 85-foot, rear-mounted Teleboom was built on a Hendrickson chassis that was delivered into the state of Florida. These units all had midship pumps and water tanks. The platform had one 1,000 gallon-per-minute monitor nozzle and a rated load capacity of 700 pounds. Stabilization was achieved with two midship-mounted H-style jacks, two downriggers behind the rear axle, and a scissors jack under the front bumper.

In 1973, Ward LaFrance and Reading Techmatic announced the Teleflow, the Telerise, and the Telelift. The Teleflow was a telescoping water tower and rescue aerial ladder, the Telerise was an articulating water tower, and the Telelift was an articulated platform aerial. The "Tele" prefix was trademarked by Snorkel, and Reading had to rename its products before they were released. Names for the products were changed to model numbers. The TWT was the telescoping water tower, the AWT was the articulating water tower, and the AWP was the articulated water platform. Snorkel also sued Reading Techmatic for patent infringement regarding design similarities with the Tele-Squrt, and a settlement was reached between the two companies. Only one of the AWP aerial devices was ever built. It was an 85-foot unit intended for Thornton, Colorado, which

was refused by the fire department. The unit was later exported in 1976 to Cartegena, Columbia. The TWT-50, a 50-foot telescoping water tower, was better received, with between 30 and 40 units produced and sold. There were a small number of TWT-55 units built and the line also offered a TWT-75, which was never built.

Reading did not have the resources to build all of the products that it had promised to Ward LaFrance, and the relationship between the two companies began to sour. Ward LaFrance was sold in 1976 and the same company purchased Maxim, bringing the companies together, while at the same ending the relationship with Reading Techmatic.

The Fox Lake Fire Department in Lake County, Illinois, received the first 75-foot, midship, Teleboom aerial platform built by Reading Techmatic under license for Ward LaFrance. The chassis was a Ford CT900 with a tandem rear axle. This unit was intended to compete with the Aerialscope but resulted in only two sales through Ward LaFrance.

American LaFrance (ALF)

In the early 1980s, American LaFrance hired an engineer to design an 80-foot, rear-mounted ladder tower to mount on a single-axle pumper chassis. A prototype of this three-section unit was built and displayed at a trade show. The jacking system proved to be complicated and the unit was overweight and impractical. The prototype was never sold and was eventually scrapped. This was in the works at a time when the FDNY was purchasing its fleet of pumpers from American LaFrance. It is possible that this unit was meant to entice the FDNY into purchasing the aerial device from American LaFrance instead of purchasing the Aerialscope, which was FDNY's exclusive tower ladder device.

In 1986, American LaFrance revamped the Century Series and announced the Century 2000 Series. Like the Century Series, this new cab offered a wide, contoured design that flared out behind the front doors for added crew space. It was available as a two-door cab with an open rear canopy, or as a four-door, fully enclosed cab. These were easily distinguished from the Century Series by the modern square headlight bezels below matching housings for turn signals and warning lights. These replaced the traditional double round headlight and warning light housings. The Century 2000 Series cab and body were made of stainless steel. The first two Century 2000 cabs and bodies were built on Spartan chassis, and then Pemfab built the chassis and drive trains for several units before HME built the remainder. At the same time, the Pacemaker Series was still available featuring custom cabs and chassis from other manufacturers. The Pioneer Series had been discontinued by this time.

Available aerials included the 75-foot Water-Chief with a 500-gallon water capacity. The 100-foot, rear-mounted

CHAPTER THREE

THE

1980s

In 1984, Pierce entered into an exclusive agreement with Smeal of Snyder, Nebraska, replacing LTI as the builder of ladders to be marketed under the Pierce name. One of the first units was this 75-foot quint for Pantego, Texas. Unlike prior arrangements with LTI, the new ladders carried the Pierce name.

Ladder-Chief and Water-Chief were similar to previous models that offered single rear axles and a choice of center or side stacked ground-ladder storage. The 100-foot, rear-mounted Ladder-Chief Quint and Water-Chief Quint were built with the previous specifications. The 100-foot, midship-mounted Ladder-Chief straight or quint was now available with an optional tandem rear axle and high side compartments. The 100-foot TDA Ladder-Chief was offered with several new options. First was the pre-piped waterway, which made it a TDA Water-Chief.

This is a 1983 American LaFrance Century Series 75-foot Water-Chief Quint that was part of the fleet in Lemont, Illinois. The pre-piped waterway consisted of dual piping on the outside of the ladder. Placement of the piping on the sides, instead of underneath, allowed for a lower travel height.

Grumman Emergency Products had an OEM agreement to market the Boardman Readi-Tower T55 telescoping water tower for a short time between 1982 and 1985. This 1985 unit from the Harvey Volunteer Fire Company 2 in Louisiana features a Duplex D350 cab and chassis. Without close examination, the unit could be confused with a Tele-Squrt from Snorkel.

Hydraulic jacks and an enclosed tillerman's cab became standard. Fifty-foot and 75-foot Tele-Squrts were part of the line-up, as well as an 85-foot, Snorkel articulating aerial platform with a 900-pound capacity.

In 1989, ALF introduced the all-new, 75-foot Water-Chief II. Both the ladder and the water system were redesigned. It offered a 500-pound tip capacity while flowing 1,000 gallons of water per minute, plus the ability to position the nozzle at 90 degrees to the ladder. Two underbody A-style jacks supported the aerial with a 13-foot jack spread. The body was made of 304 stainless steel mounted on a Century 2000 pumper chassis with a two-door or four-door cab, a 500-gallon water tank, and a 1,500 gallon-per-minute pump. Both the stainless steel body and the heavier ladder made the vehicle very heavy for a singe-axle chassis. ALF sold less than five of the Water-Chief II aerials.

All of these enhancements and modifications were not enough to continue the lifeblood of one of the oldest and

longest running names in fire apparatus. American LaFrance closed its doors in 1994.

Boardman

Readi-Tower units were now being sold through OEM alliances with Boardman, Emergency One, Grumman, Towers, and Superior out of Canada. In 1981, the T50 product was reintroduced as a T55, in hopes of getting a leg up on Snorkel by offering a longer length. An A61 special order articulating water tower was designed for use by the New Orleans Fire Department, but it never found any other buyers.

In 1983, the Readi-Tower Corporation was dissolved and the aerial operations came under the Boardman brand, still using the Readi-Tower name. Readi-Tower still sold aerial devices through OEM manufacturers, although some preferred not to buy from a competitor. Readi-Tower devices were ordered by Boardman, 3D, Towers, and one unit was built on a pumper and sold by Pirsch to the fire

This is an example from 1981 of an early version of the 55-foot StratoSpear telescoping boom from Emergency One. Built on a Ford C-Series chassis for Canon City, Colorado, the unit has one set of A-style jacks located behind the rear axle.

department in Oak Brook, Illinois. The T55 accounted for better than 85 percent of all aerial product sales for Boardman, although the 75-foot water tower as well as the 50-foot and 61-foot articulating boom water towers were still available.

In 1990, Boardman Fire Apparatus was offering a complete package unit with a 55-foot water tower on a Spartan chassis priced very competitively as a means to increase sales.

In the early 1990s, the Readi-Tower name disappeared from the aerial products in favor of the Apache designation. The Apache Aerials included the T-55, 55-foot Apache telescoping ladder; the T-75, 75-foot Apache telescoping ladder; and the Apache 61-foot articulating boom.

In 1995, the Boardman fire division was liquidated. The last T-55 built by Boardman went to Glenview, Illinois in 1995 on an HME chassis with bodywork by Luverne. Aerial Innovations purchased the aerial operations and Sinor Manufacturing purchased the fire apparatus line. Sinor built rescues and ambulances under the Boardman name until it became part of the new American LaFrance family that reemerged in 1999.

Emergency One

The first aerial device designed exclusively for Emergency One in 1980 was a 65-foot, box boom, telescoping water tower. One was built and then the unit was changed, becoming a 55-foot unit titled the StratoSpear 55-foot telescoping boom. Designed to compete with the Tele-Squrt from Snorkel, the two-section boom was aluminum with a

two-section, aluminum ladder permanently attached to the boom sections for rescue capabilities. Two waterways, one mounted on either side of the boom, supplied the hydraulically controlled nozzle at the tip and two rear-mounted A-style jacks supported the unit. Boom and nozzle controls were located at the rear of the apparatus and were utilized by standing on the rear step. The telescoping boom could be mounted to either a commercial or custom pumper chassis with a single or tandem rear axle. The pumper was built with a Hale pump and a choice of water tanks that ranged from 300 to 500 gallons. The fire department in Syracuse, New York, purchased several of these units on Spartan Maxi-Vision chassis in the early 1980s.

At the same time, Emergency One also formed an OEM alliance with Simon Aerials, the North American distributor for Simon Engineering, a British company that built fire apparatus and aerial devices overseas. Emergency One began marketing the Simon Snorkel in the United States as part of its aerial line, though the company did not have exclusive rights to the product in the United States. This device was a three-boom, rear-mounted, articulating aerial device with a basket at the end and an aluminum ladder along the boom sections. Emergency One called it the StratoSpear 103-foot articulating platform. The capacity was 800 pounds in the platform, and Emergency One mounted the units that were sold in the United States on low-profile Hendrickson tandem-axle chassis. Simon used four A-style outriggers, and the aerials were offered with a water tank and midship Hale fire pump. Emergency One sold approximately 20 of these units with the first going to the fire department in Clearwater, Florida. Emergency One also offered a 77-foot version of the Simon Snorkel, shipping several to the Middle East mounted on Pemfab Wedge chassis. The Simon Snorkel did not prove to be popular with the American fire market.

In 1982, Emergency One introduced the four-section, 110-foot, all-welded extruded aluminum StratoSpear aerial. In design, the unit was basically an aluminum Fire Spire. Although the aluminum construction required thicker sections, it was roughly one-third lighter in weight. The StratoSpear was designed to compete with the Fire Spire and it had an additional 4 feet of reach. The tip load was 200 pounds and there was an option for a pre-piped waterway. When it was released, the StratoSpear 110-foot aerial ladder was the tallest ladder made in the United States. As with everything that Emergency One built from aluminum, the ladder was advertised to be inherently resistant to corrosion. Initially designed around and built only on a wide, aluminum 1871-W Hendrickson chassis, this aerial also introduced a new torque box developed with Hendrickson. The torque box was integral with the chassis frame, as opposed to other designs that rested on top of, and were subsequently bolted to the chassis frame rails. This design allowed for integral structural support with the chassis, a lower center of gravity for the unit, and improved stability for cornering. It was also the only American aerial ladder using an underslung, crisscross or scissors–style jack system for support, based on a design commonly used in the crane industry. Although this jack system was more complicated and difficult to build than H-style outriggers, the narrower spread and the low center of gravity was a benefit that Emergency One wanted to offer. The jack spread, as determined for each aerial device, is a function of the gross vehicle weight and the rated overturning moment of the

machine. Hence, the lighter weight ladder required less counter balance or jack spread to maintain the stability factor. Due to the minimal jack spread, 11 feet, and the low nature of the underslung jacks, Emergency One eliminated the need for short-jacking operations—necessary when there is not enough room to fully extend wider-spread stabilizers with larger H-style outriggers. This benefit could save both time and effort at the fire scene.

The 110-foot aerial could be built with a long list of options including two other Hendrickson cabs, as well as pumps and 200-gallon water tanks to make a quint. When configured with a pump and tank, the unit utilized a tandem axle while single or tandem axles could be requested when ordering a 110-foot aerial without a pump.

This was the first unit in a family of ladders that were designed to share components. Within a matter of years, the family would include the 200-pound, medium-duty 110-foot; a 400-pound, heavy-duty 110-foot; a 200-pound 135-foot; an 800-pound, 95-foot aerial platform; and a 400-pound, 80-foot aerial ladder.

In 1983, Emergency One introduced the three-section, 80-foot, StratoSpear aerial ladder, which was first shown on the Spartan CFC2000 chassis. This 400-pound tip-load aerial was offered on a single-axle pumper chassis and utilized two rear-mounted, underslung scissors jacks with a 13-foot spread that were bolted to the chassis. This bolt-on torque box system was different from the integral design used by the 110-foot model. Controls for the aerial and the pre-piped waterway were located at the pump panel. There was no console at the turntable. The aerial was basically the 110-foot ladder without the fly section.

The Orange County, Florida, fire department purchased one of the first 110-foot StratoSpear aerial ladders with a pre-piped waterway from Emergency One in 1982. The unit had a pump and water tank. It was built on a Hendrickson 1871-W Series chassis with an integral torque box designed by Emergency One and Hendrickson engineers. The waterway nozzle was protected by an aluminum housing that allowed the ladder to be placed against a building without causing damage to the nozzle or piping.

In 1983, Emergency One introduced the StratoSpear 95-foot aerial platform. The first unit built on a Pemfab Maxi-944-T chassis was delivered as a full quint to the Trail Park Fire Department in Palm Beach County, Florida.

Also in 1983, Emergency One entered into the aerial platform market with the StratoSpear 95-foot aerial platform. This was a three-section ladder with an 800-pound-capacity platform that measured 15 square feet. Like the 110-foot ladder, it used four underslung jacks with a 13-foot spread—subsequently increased to 13 feet, 8 inches for improved stability. As with all platform aerials, this one required a tandem-axle custom chassis. It was built originally on the Pemfab Maxi 944-T as a full quint with a pump and 200-gallon water tank. As an option, Emergency One offered water tanks holding up to 750 gallons with diminished space for ground ladders. Standard construction offered a single monitor nozzle in the center of the platform.

In 1984, the next ladder that was added to the family was the five-section, 135-foot StratoSpear aerial ladder, which replaced the 110-foot model as the tallest ladder built in the United States. The original unit had a 200-pound tip capacity and was built on a tandem-axle Pemfab Royale S942-T chassis as a quint with a 200-gallon water tank and a pre-piped waterway that stopped at the tip of the fourth fly section. Emergency One offered an optional water tank with a capacity of up to 500 gallons and reduced space for ladder storage. The four underslung scissors jacks had a 13-foot, 8-inch spread.

Also in 1984, Emergency One offered a 100-foot aerial platform. This was similar in all aspects to the 95-foot model except for a reduced, 700-pound capacity. The 100-foot model never went into production.

The family of aerials shared common components that required slight modifications to produce the various ladders. The 110-foot medium-duty used the upper four sections of the 135-foot. The 110-foot heavy-duty used the lower four sections of the 135-foot, and the 95-foot platform used the lower three sections of the 135-foot with a bucket attached. The 80-foot used the bottom three sections of the 110-foot (slightly shortened) or the middle three sections of the 135-foot.

The big news in 1984 was Emergency One's entrance into the custom chassis market. Intent on taking the market by storm, the company revealed the Hurricane. This new chassis featured an all-aluminum cab with a 1/4-inch-thick outer shell, thicker than other custom cab manufacturers were making. Originally offered in a squared design with a large, flat face and single-piece windshield, the Hurricane was available for pumpers, tankers, and aerials. Emergency One released a contoured version of the Hurricane with a two-piece, curved windshield shortly thereafter.

Within a year, Emergency One had spun off the chassis production to a new sister company that utilized facilities on the same property in Ocala, Florida. Federal Motors was incorporated in 1985, and tasked with supplying Emergency One with the Hurricane chassis as well as venturing for a short time into other markets for custom chassis. Federal Motors built four- and six-wheel-drive chassis for utility applications and drill rigs, and designed its own trolley bus, the Hurricane Express, for public transportation in tourist areas.

In the ensuing years, the company dropped the StratoSpear designation in favor of the more simply stated Emergency One Aerial System, and began to use E-ONE over the full name. The company built a new aerial in the mid-1980s, reportedly at the request of a handful of dealers who expressed a need and an extensive prospective market. The product was a 96-foot, midship-mounted aerial ladder on an E-ONE Hurricane custom chassis with a square, two-door cab. This unit had no pump or water tank and was essentially a 110-foot unit that was shortened to achieve the needed travel length and stability. It had four sections, a

200-pound tip load, and shared the outriggers and bolt-on torque box with the 80-foot rear-mount aerial. Only two units were ever built and they were delivered to departments in Halifax and Quincy, Massachusetts. The midship aerial was discontinued in 1991.

E-ONE again surprised the market in 1985 by introducing the next generation custom chassis called the Hush. This model had the engine mounted to the rear of the chassis frame, thereby accomplishing several tasks, the most important of which was to reduce the engine noise in the cab. In addition to creating a quieter cab, the interior was much roomier without the doghouse, or engine compartment, between the firefighters. This design included seating options for up to nine firefighters. Several cab configurations were offered with differing rear doors, depending on the length of the cab ordered. To further reduce the noise inside the cab, air horns and sirens were removed from the roof and mounted behind the front bumper. Cutout sections along the front of the bumper directed the noise forward into traffic. Red lights were added to the interior to reduce the sudden change in light levels when persons exit the vehicle at night. The Hush was also the first model available solely as a fully enclosed cab.

The aerial program at this time consisted of rear-mounted, straight aerial ladders in 80-foot, 110-foot, and 135-foot lengths; a 95-foot platform; and the 55-foot telescoping boom. The straight ladders were offered in each size with or without pumps, and the 110-foot was offered with a 200-pound tip load or a heavy-duty, 400-pound tip load. Standard water tanks for the 80-foot aerials were 300 gallons, and 200 gallons for the 110-foot ladders, 135-foot aerial, and for the platform. Jack spread was 13 feet for the 80-foot; 11 feet for the 200-pound 110-foot; and 13 feet, 8 inches for the heavy-duty 110-foot, the 135-foot aerial, and the 95-foot platform. The two-section, 55-foot telescoping boom, offered on commercial or custom chassis, had a 9-foot, 10-inch jack spread and was available with either a 300- or 500-gallon water tank on varying wheelbases.

In 1987, the bucket for the platform aerial was redesigned using an aircraft-style riveted skin with squared panels in place of rounded sides. The waterway piping was re-routed around the base of the bucket and became part of the structural support of the platform. This new design raised the bottom of the bucket, which improved driver visibility when the platform was bedded. The new platform offered 16 square feet of space. During 1987 the last E-ONE aerials, excluding the telescoping boom and Snorkel

products, were built on non–E-ONE chassis. From that point forward, the entire family of aerials was offered exclusively on the company's own custom chassis.

The Hush Series was initially released as a pumper and subsequently adapted for rescue vehicles. At the time of the Hush chassis' release, the aerial designers were modifying the telescoping boom to accommodate midship mounting compatible with the Hush's rear engine placement. By 1988, the Hush Series included a 50-foot telescoping boom called the Teleboom. This was essentially a pumper capable of carrying 300 or 500 gallons of water in addition to the aerial device. The two A-style jacks were moved to the middle of the unit, beneath the aerial turntable, and maintained the same spread of 9 feet, 10 inches. This version became a three-section device with a waterway and a telescoping

Emergency One added the StratoSpear 80-foot ladder in 1983, and in 1984 the company unveiled the Hurricane custom fire truck chassis. Parker, Colorado, received two aerials on Hurricane chassis in 1984, including this 80-foot ladder, which is a quint with a tandem rear axle. Without a protective guard at the tip of the fly section, the department has to exercise caution to avoid damaging the waterway when placing the ladder against a building.

aluminum rescue ladder and was rated with a 400-pound tip load. The 50-foot model was lighter in weight than the previous two-section, 55-foot model adapted from the original 65-foot design. When the 65-foot model was paired down to 55 feet, the new item was overbuilt and heavier than necessary for a 55-foot unit. Access to the new ladder was via a vertical ladder built directly behind the cab. The 50-foot unit was also offered as a rear-mounted device for other E-ONE or commercial chassis. This three-section model was shorter than the 50-foot unit offered by the competition. The 50-foot E-ONE had a new tuck-away nozzle and a different looking rounded design at the tip of the waterway.

In 1988, Chicago purchased its second five-section, 135-foot, E-ONE aerial. It was configured without a pump or water tank in a way that is common to larger cities. This truck featured a fully enclosed, contoured Hurricane cab unlike the square design that was originally introduced.

Later in the same year, the Teleboom was adapted and made available as an option on the Titan crash, firefighting and rescue (CFR) vehicles to be deployed at airports. The first such unit was shipped to the West Palm Beach Florida Airport. Perhaps only three of these devices were eventually utilized for aircraft equipment. Most airports did not require an aerial device rated to carry a man, instead a lighter weight, remote controlled waterway was favored.

The family of aerials did not change significantly in 1988, but E-ONE did introduce its third custom chassis, the Cyclone. All of the chassis were now offered with fully enclosed four-door versions as the fire service had begun to adopt this style to provide comfort and safety for firefighters. The 80-foot aerial came standard as a quint and was no longer offered without a pump. There were no changes for either of the 110-foot models or the 135-foot model, except

that the Cyclone became an option for the 110-foot aerial with a pump. As an aside, the 110-foot heavy-duty aerial was never a big seller, with less than 20 units built.

In 1989, E-ONE introduced a three-section, 75-foot aerial to replace the 80-foot. The ladder was optimized with relation to the weight of the ladder and its length. The 80-foot aerial with its 250-pound tip load had been overbuilt. The new aerial had two rear underslung criss-cross scissors jacks with a 13-foot spread, more compartment space, up to a 500-gallon water tank, and the same bolt-on torque box. Whereas the 80-foot was rated for two people at the tip, the 75-foot had a one-person tip. The 80-foot also allowed only 300 gallons of water. The 75-foot was available on the Hurricane, Hurricane mid-engine, Hush mid-engine, Cyclone mid-engine, Cyclone Tilt, or the Protector chassis.

The Fire Apparatus Division of FMC had an OEM agreement with LTI for many years. This 1982 aerial for Rochester, Minnesota, was sold by FMC but was built in the Conestoga plant at LTI. The CFPC3064 chassis by Spartan was part of the Maxi-Vision Series. The fly section of the ladder was extended to protect the nozzle.

FMC

In the early 1980s, the Fire Apparatus Division of FMC marketed a full line of aerials to complement its pumpers. FMC had an OEM alliance with LTI to market 50-foot through 100-foot steel aerial ladders and ladder towers. Since FMC only built fire pumps and pumper bodies, a customer would first specify a custom fire truck chassis from Duplex, Hendrickson, Pemfab, or Spartan, which would travel to the FMC facility in Tipton, Indiana. Once there, FMC would mount an FMC Ram or Hale fire pump. Then the rig would be sent to LTI to have the torque box, outriggers, and aerial device mounted. Next, the unit would have a body built by Conestoga Custom Products, the LTI body company, and be adorned with FMC nameplates. Although few FMC aerial units were produced, only one featured a body that was built by FMC. That unit went to McAllen, Texas, in 1984 with an MZ-100 LTI tower, ladder, and serial number 8402818.

Customers could choose from an 85-foot or 100-foot ladder tower, 75-foot Aqua Stix, 55-foot water tower, or a 100-foot aerial ladder. Towers offered center or side stack ladder storage, 2,000 gallon-per-minute output from the platform, four H-style outriggers with a 16-foot or 18-foot spread, 17 square feet of space in the platform, and 1,900 pounds or 2,500 pounds of distributed load for the 85-foot and 100-foot models respectively.

The Aqua Stix was a three-section, rear- or midship-mounted aerial with a 2,000-pound distributed load, a 16-foot jack spread with two outriggers, and aerial controls placed at the pump panel and the tip of the ladder.

The water tower was a small, two-section, telescoping boom with an aluminum rescue ladder along the top. Two A-style jacks stabilized the unit. Ladder elevation was accomplished with a single hydraulic cylinder, where all other products used two cylinders. The water tower had a 1,000 gallon-per-minute output, controlled at the ladder's tip or at the pump panel.

The rear-mounted, midship-mounted, or TDAs had four sections with a distributed load rating of 1,500 pounds. They utilized four H-style outriggers with a 16-foot spread, and were available with a pinnable, pre-piped waterway. No TDAs were sold by FMC.

Around 1981, FMC had a desire to enter into the aerial ladder market with an exclusive product. The company wanted to develop a ladder tower that could also be built as a straight aerial ladder. The Fire Apparatus Division invested in the research and development of this new product through the Link-Belt crane division of FMC in Lexington, Kentucky, which specialized in building booms and long

The Wayne Township Fire Department in Indiana purchased this unique aerial ladder prototype in 1985. FMC had tried to enter the aerial ladder market with an exclusive line of aerials and contracted with Firefab for design, engineering, and fabrication. After building the prototype, differences between the companies forced FMC not to pursue production of this aerial product line and it remains a one-of-a-kind aerial. The low-profile chassis is a Duplex D450.

reach devices for the construction industry. Between 1981 and 1983, the Link-Belt Division did not make tremendous progress in the development of an aerial. The division planned to use a solid, closed boom section design similar to the hydraulic cranes that it built, unlike the open designs of aerials in the fire industry. The Fire Apparatus Division had spent considerable time and money to this point on an aerial program that seemed to be going nowhere.

At that point, The Fire Apparatus Division hired a structural engineer with previous experience designing fire service aerials as a consultant to evaluate the program being designed by Link-Belt. After his examination, the program was terminated. The consultant, Bob Vanstone, was then hired to oversee a new design. Prototype fabrication was subcontracted to the Hahn Company service organization. FMC acquired the old Reading Techmatic facility in Reading, Pennsylvania, and fabricated the prototype ladder tower on a low-profile D-450 Duplex chassis. This unit consisted of a chassis, cab, torque box, outriggers, and aerial device with no body. It was displayed at the 1985 IAFC convention in New Orleans and then at the Fire Expo in Baltimore. It had a four-section ladder, a 1,000-pound capacity with 1,000 gallons of water flowing through a pre-piped waterway, a reach of 102 feet, and used four H-style outriggers.

Market analysis by FMC suggested a low probability of making money and recouping its investments with this new aerial, considering the other established manufacturers and the size of the market. The cost of the program proved prohibitive and the aerial tower never went into production. Although they were successful in designing a strong product, FMC engineers were disappointed with the prototype. The unit was not built with the proper tubing, or with other materials required by the design specifications. FMC

decided that the unit could not be placed into service, and the ladder was removed from the chassis and cut up as scrap.

In 1986, FMC moved the Fire Apparatus Division from Tipton, Indiana, to an FMC facility in Orlando, Florida. There it shared production space with another division that made specialized equipment for moving cargo and luggage at airports. Once again, FMC tried to enter the aerial ladder market on its own. Within the next year, FMC enlisted the help of the former Steeldraulics designers that produced the first AerialCat towers for Grumman. Under the name of Firefab, it had designs for a line of five aerial products. The first to be manufactured was a four-section, 102-foot, rearmounted, steel aerial ladder prototype. This aerial also used four H-style outriggers and was mounted on the Duplex chassis that previously had the ladder tower prototype. The aerial also received a 1,200 gallon-per-minute pump and a 300-gallon water tank. After building the prototype, differences between the companies led FMC to abandon this aerial product line and it remains a one-of-a-kind aerial. FMC built a body around the unit and the Wayne Township Fire Department in Indiana purchased it.

This marked the end of FMC's quest to add aerials to its product mix. FMC concentrated on commercial and custom pumpers for the next several years until the Fire Apparatus Division was shut down in 1990.

Grumman

Howe Fire Apparatus offered aerial ladders and tower ladders built by Grove in the early 1970s, and was an OEM distributor of LTI products after that company acquired Grove's aerial manufacturing in 1974. Grumman Emergency Products was born of an acquisition of the Howe Fire Apparatus Company in 1976, which had merged with Coast

The first Grumman AerialCat platform aerial was built in 1982 and sold to the Friendship Fire and Hose Company of Elizabethtown, Pennsylvania. Steeldraulics, a company formed by former LTI employees, built this truck for Grumman. The unit pictured here received certain structural modifications after delivery to coincide with upgrades that were recommended by the Aerospace Division of Grumman, following extensive testing. The most obvious of the modifications were the force distribution members on the base section behind the letters "ABET".

Apparatus in 1965, and Oren Fire Apparatus in 1961. Grumman consolidated the Howe facility in Anderson, Indiana, with the Oren facility in Roanoke, Virginia, and eventually closed the Coast facility in California. Grumman was a body builder specializing in pumpers using commercial or custom fire truck chassis built by others. With the acquisition of Howe, Grumman became an OEM distributor for LTI. In the early 1980s, the relationship between Grumman and LTI was terminated. LTI decided that it would concentrate on Pierce and FMC as its two major OEMs. An engineer who had left LTI prior to this time designed a ladder tower with components similar to those used by LTI. He formed a company called Steeldraulics and entered into talks with Grumman about producing aerials for them. The initial design was only on paper. Grumman provided funding for six of these aerials to be built by Steeldraulics.

Grumman entered the aerial market in 1982 with the AerialCat ladder tower. This was the first aerial platform to challenge the LTI tower that had been available through several OEMs since 1974. Outwardly, the AerialCat towers differed very little from the LTI. The first five were sold to the Friendship Fire and Hose Company of Elizabethtown, Pennsylvania; Monterey Park, California; Palo Alto, California; East Lansing, Michigan; and Vails Gate, New York. Since they were purchasing prototype units, these fire departments were promised that to whatever degree was possible, their aerials would be upgraded should further design elements be added to the AerialCat. The units were built on different chassis. The first in 1982, for Elizabethtown, was built on a Duplex D400 chassis without a pump or water tank. The others came out in 1983. The unit for Monterey Park was a quint on a Hendrickson 1871C chassis, and the Vails Gate quint was on a Duplex D350 chassis with a standard-height cab. The Palo Alto AerialCat was built on a low-profile Duplex D450 chassis and was built without a water tank and pump. The AerialCat quint for East Lansing, just outside the home of Spartan Motors, a custom fire truck chassis company, was built on a Spartan CFC3064 chassis.

Originally introduced as a 95-foot tower, the AerialCat had an unrestricted 750-pound weight rating with an output of 1,500 gallons per minute from the platform. A Waterous 1,250 or 1,500 gallon-per-minute pump was

The majority of Grumman AerialCat platform aerials were built on Duplex, Spartan, or Panther chassis. One of the few unique configurations built was this 102-foot unit in 1985 for Broadview, Illinois, on an American LaFrance low-profile Century Series chassis. The engineering involved to build on different chassis caused Grumman to refuse further special requests.

available along with a 200-gallon water tank. Bodies were made of galvaneal steel on Duplex, Hendrickson, Pemfab, or Spartan chassis. The three-section ladder was steel and the platform was aluminum, offering 15 square feet of space. Ground-ladder storage was available in the center of the body with high side compartments, or side stacked above low side compartments. Side stacking was generally used to lower the travel height of the truck. The AerialCat used four H-style outriggers with an 18-foot spread and featured two double acting lift cylinders.

During this time, Grumman purchased the aerial design and decided to send the sixth unit for comprehensive testing. Taking full advantage of the resources available to them as part of Grumman, the Emergency Products Division sent the sixth AerialCat to the Commercial Development Center (CDC) in Bohemia, Long Island. This was the same facility that performed testing for the Aerospace Division on the F14 Tomcat fighter jets that were built by Grumman for the U.S. Navy.

As the story goes, the engineers were unfamiliar with the ladder tower and asked what they were to test for. In order to gain an insight into the appropriate test criteria, they inquired as to the use these truss design aerials experienced in the fire service. They questioned whether the aerial could be used in high winds and if it were possible to use

an aerial in icy conditions as well. The engineers put the device through a rigorous program that included strain gauge testing and measurement of side loads. In their subsequent report to the Emergency Products Division, the engineers said that the ladder failed to meet their requirements. Grumman then modified the design, specifying increased metal thickness, increased handrail height on the fly section, and the addition of seven steel plates welded vertically to each side of the base ladder section. These were called "Force Distribution Members" and were intended to distribute the stress from the

weakest point of the ladder to the strongest point, which was the side plates of the base ladder section. As these changes were implemented, the first five AerialCats were retrofitted with the Force Distribution Members and strengthening of the base sections.

In addition to the design changes that emerged from the CDC, the aerospace engineers developed a unique proof load test for truss design ladders. The first step was to tie the front of the chassis down to the ground. Next, depending on the model of the aerial, as much as 4,877 pounds was hung off the ladder straight off the back of the truck at a zero-degree elevation to pre-stress the welds. This weight was divided over the three sections as follows: 1,642 pounds on the fly section, 1,468 pounds on the mid section, and the 1,767-pound remaining balance on the base section. The weight was achieved by filling specially designed containers with water. Every AerialCat ladder underwent this testing before delivery and at recommended intervals throughout the life of the aerial while it was in service.

The majority of AerialCats over the years were built on Duplex chassis. Several Spartans were ordered, as few as two Hendricksons were ever built, and perhaps only one Pemfab was built. One other unique AerialCat was built in 1985 for the Broadview, Illinois, fire department on an American LaFrance low-profile Century Series chassis. Grumman shied away from building on other chassis due to the increased time and money involved to accomplish the necessary engineering with each new chassis.

Also in 1982, Grumman expanded its aerial product offerings through an agreement to market devices built by Boardman (in addition to the Fire Spire that it had been offering from Hahn since 1977). The Boardman products were the 55-foot and 75-foot Readi-Tower units. These were elevated master stream devices with a telescopic, aluminum rescue ladder. The Readi-Tower was built to compete with the Tele-Squrt from Snorkel. The Hahn Fire Spire aerial ladders were offered in lengths of 85 feet and 106 feet as rear-mounts. These were available on single- or tandem-axle chassis and used four A-style outrigger jacks for support.

In 1983, the modified AerialCat tower was released. In addition to the Force Distribution Members, the base ladder section had been increased in size. Before production was moved from the Steeldraulics facilities to Grumman in Roanoke, Virginia, eight more units were manufactured.

In 1985, another AerialCat tower was released—a 102-foot model with an 800-pound rating. At the same time, the

In 1987, Grumman entered into the mid-mount platform aerial market with the 92-foot AerialCat. The low travel height translated into less compartment space for equipment because designers had to mount the ladder lower to the frame. The small ladders for climbing into the platform proved to be cumbersome and awkward while driving. These were not included on subsequent units. Grumman also placed the pump at the rear of the unit, differing from other mid-mount units of the time by Sutphen and Baker. The unit went to the Thompsonville Fire Company Number 1 in Enfield, Connecticut.

In 1987, Grumman released a mid-mounted AerialCat platform. Built on a two-door, flat-faced, Spartan Gladiator chassis. This 92-foot, four-section, steel aerial platform rode on a tandem-axle chassis with four H-style outriggers, and was the first mid-mounted ladder tower to compete with the Sutphen tower for customers that had older firehouses with 10-foot clearance into the station. Since the Sutphen tower featured a box construction, Grumman's design was in a class by itself and offered the full ladder up to the platform. Unique to this model was the placement of the pump at the rear of the unit with the operator's panel at the rear on the driver's side. The pump was hydraulically driven, giving the operator a quiet environment away from the noise of the engine. Due to the low clearance of this unit, ground ladders were stacked on the sides of the body, over the low side compartments. The platform was rated to carry 1,000 pounds. The first unit also had small ladders on each side of the platform. Again, this was to compete with the Sutphen rigs, which offered easy entry into the platform from the ground while the aerial was bedded. As it turned out, these ladders created maneuverability problems, when making tight corners. Fire departments were content to access the platform by simply climbing up on the rear of the apparatus, eliminating the concerns caused by the two side ladders. After the first unit, the ladders were no longer part of the mid-mount design. The first unit was sold to the Thompsonville Fire Department, Ladder Company 1, of Enfield, Connecticut, with a 1,500 gallon-per-minute pump and a 200-gallon water tank. In 1988, the mid-mount was modified with the addition of one downrigger placed in the center of the cab face to increase the working range of the aerial. The mid-mount unit was not as popular as Grumman had hoped, and less than 10 were built.

weight rating for the 95-foot model was increased to 1,000 pounds. The proof load testing for the 95-foot AerialCat remained the same but the 102-foot model was tested with 4,677 pounds. The AerialCats featured a 3:1 safety factor. Bodybuilding was modified to include an aluminum option but all other characteristics remained the same. Additional options included single or dual turrets in the platform for master stream operations. AerialCats were purchased primarily on low-profile chassis, but many were also built on standard cab height units. Both versions were also purchased with conventional two-door cabs and with four-door, fully enclosed cabs. The low-profile cabs almost always were built with a raised roof section above the rear jump seats whether they were open or enclosed. Virtually all of the AerialCats were produced as full quints with fire pumps and water tanks, but a rare few were built as straight trucks with additional compartment storage space such as the first units for Elizabethtown, Pennsylvania, and Palo Alto, California. Other non-quint AerialCats went to the Deer Park Fire Company in Cherry Hill, New Jersey; Arlington, Virginia; and two units for the District of Columbia Fire Department.

Also in 1985, Grumman became an authorized OEM with Snorkel. They replaced the Readi-Tower products with Tele-Squrts and added the Snorkel articulating elevating platforms. The Tele-Squrts were mounted on FireCat pumpers and were available at the time in 50-foot and 75-foot lengths. The Snorkels were available in 55-, 75-, and 85-foot sizes and were capable of putting out a 1,000 gallon-per-minute master stream.

Also in 1987, Grumman began developing a new ladder. The company secured a design from an outside engineer, which the company then modified and completed in-house. In 1988, Grumman announced the result—a 110-foot, rear-mounted straight stick aerial. This was a four-section, steel aerial with a rating of 500 pounds.

Like the AerialCat tower, this new ladder utilized four H-style outriggers and required a tandem-axle chassis. Grumman management thoroughly reviewed the ladder after the prototype was built and concluded that it was not a viable product. It was extremely labor intensive with an excessive number of parts requiring too much welding. Only the one unit was built and was delivered in December of 1988 to the fire department in Macon, Georgia.

In 1988, more Grumman customers were looking to purchase a straight stick, rear-mounted aerial ladder. Since the 110-foot ladder was not available, Grumman had to pursue other options. The Grumman reputation was based on high performance, heavy-duty aerials. Grumman did not want to produce a light-duty or medium-duty ladder, so the company needed to come up with another heavy-duty unit. Complicating matters was the fact that any new product had to undergo extensive and rigorous supplemental testing through the CDC before the corporate office would allow its release for sale. The testing was both a difficult and time-consuming process. Grumman Emergency Products went to corporate management and pointed out that the design for the AerialCat tower had already been tested and approved. It was further suggested that the bucket should be removed to produce a straight aerial ladder. Grumman then started with a 102-foot, rear-mounted aerial platform, removed the basket and the support arms, and ended up with a 95-foot straight aerial. Except for the bucket, this product was in all other aspects the same as an aerial platform. The aerial featured a pre-piped waterway that nested beneath the fly section. The ladder was rated with a 1,000-pound tip load, when in actuality the amount of weight it could handle was considerably more since it was designed to have a 1,000-pound capacity plus the added weight of a platform. However, there was no need at the time to issue a higher tip load when it would be impractical to assume that much weight would ever be at the tip. It was an expensive aerial ladder when compared to the competition, which offered 500-pound tip loads, and few were built. The first went to Niceville, Florida, in February of 1989 and was followed in September of that year with another unit going to Franklin, Virginia.

Grumman wanted to supply a straight aerial ladder to fulfill customer requests and had logistics problems with a new design the company developed in 1987. Instead, Grumman decided to remove the platform from the 102-foot AerialCat and offer a 95-foot, super heavy-duty ladder. Sharing all of the other characteristics with the platform aerial, this unit was expensive and resulted in few sales.

Following the 95-foot ladder, Grumman dealers wanted a 100-foot ladder to compete head-on with other companies in that market. Again, the Emergency Products Division went to corporate seeking to extend the ladder sections of the 95-foot to achieve the 100-foot length without having to go through re-approval and retesting. In May of 1990, the first 100-foot straight stick ladder was sold to the Westlake Fire Department in Erie, Pennsylvania. The fire department in Hamilton, Ontario, Canada, wanted to purchase a 100-foot ladder and required that it be subjected to testing by Underwriter's Laboratory (U.L.) of Canada. All U.S. aerials were certified by U.L. testing in the states, but the Canadian standards were more rigid. Grumman agreed to the testing and this became the first U.S.-built ladder to pass Canadian U.L. review. The ladder was delivered in November of 1991.

In 1988, Grumman designed an exclusive cab and chassis that it would offer to its customers. Initially, Grumman made the first cab shells and the chassis. The cabs were then sent to Spartan for wiring, upholstery, glass, and the balance of the trim items. Upon completion, the cabs were returned to Grumman for mounting on the chassis. This arrangement only lasted for a short period, at which point Grumman entered into an exclusive private label program with HME, Inc., a custom chassis maker that purchased the specialized conventional truck assets of the Hendrickson Mobile Equipment Division in 1985. The cab construction was subcontracted to TCM, and HME built the chassis and finished the cabs. This chassis was called the Panther and was available for pumpers, tankers, and aerials. From that time forward, almost all of the AerialCats produced were mounted on a Panther low-profile chassis.

Grumman introduced the 121-foot, AerialCat, rear-mounted, all-steel aerial ladder in 1989. Grumman had wanted to provide a longer steel ladder than the industry currently had to offer. Management considered that both the 110-foot and 100-foot ladders had received corporate approval and discovered that the fly section of the 110-foot would fit into the 100-foot sections with minor modifications. They asked the engineers to determine what length would result from adding a fourth ladder section to the 100-foot model. Engineers were able to successfully merge the basic design of the three-section, 100-foot ladder with the fly section from the 110-foot ladder to achieve the 121-foot length. This was rated at 250 pounds while flowing water and 500 pounds dry. Grumman now offered the tallest steel ladder/waterway in the United States. As exciting as this new introduction was, the market for this product was not strong and approximately eight were built, several of which went to Cleveland. This 121-foot ladder was offered as a straight truck design or with a pump and water tank.

In 1992, after Pentagon budget cutbacks affected Grumman's core aerospace business, the fire apparatus division of Kovatch Mobile Equipment (KME) purchased the assets to the Grumman Emergency Products Division. While the company maintained the plant in Roanoke, Virginia, to build the AerialCat ladders, the remainder of the product line was not utilized because KME already had pumpers and tankers of its own through previous acquisitions. The Grumman purchase was used to gain access to the aerial products market.

Kovatch Mobile Equipment (KME)

The Kovatch Mobile Equipment Company began producing fire apparatus in 1983. KME purchased the assets and body designs from Mack Trucks' fire apparatus division when Mack left the industry. In 1985, Kovatch purchased the custom fire truck chassis line from Hendrickson Mobile Equipment when that company exited the fire market.

KME Fire Apparatus, as the division was known, received a large contract for fire apparatus from the United States Army in 1985. During the next several years, most of KME Fire Apparatus production was devoted to fulfilling multiple military contracts.

In 1987, KME entered the aerial fire apparatus market after purchasing the 55-foot Fire Stix product from LTI. KME expanded the product line in 1988 by adding a 75-foot Fire Stix. KME was also an OEM distributor for Snorkel products.

Ladder Towers, Inc. (LTI)

In the early 1980s, FMC, Grumman, and Pierce were the primary LTI OEMs. These bigger buyers wanted exclusivity with the LTI aerial product line. Prior to this time, it was not uncommon for a fire department that was interested in buying an aerial device to receive visits from several OEM sales representatives to discuss designing an aerial. Each time a different OEM rep visited the fire department, an LTI rep would accompany him to discuss the specifics of the aerial. It became awkward for the same LTI rep to revisit the fire department with each successive OEM sales rep. In addition, for several reasons, LTI wanted to concentrate on selling ladders through a few large OEMs and to cut out most of the smaller ones. One such reason was apparent with some OEMs. For example when building the body for

In 1982, the Metro-Dade County Fire Department sponsored independent testing to verify claims made by LTI as to the capabilities of the MZ-100 tower. Satisfied with the results, Metro-Dade wanted a straight ladder as strong as the tower. LTI then introduced the ML3S-100, an MZ-100 without the platform. This had a 1,000-pound rating and maintained all of the characteristics and specifications of the ladder tower. The order was given through Pierce, which was an OEM at the time, and the units were produced in 1983 on Pierce Arrow chassis.

an aerial, it was important to have access panels to service the hydraulics. Several of the smaller companies that fabricated bodies neglected to include these panels, which meant LTI had to cut into the sheet metal for servicing.

Several changes came about in 1981. Engineers increased the platform capacity for the 100-foot ladder tower to 800 pounds dry and 600 pounds wet by changing the extension cylinder design. In addition, the outrigger stance was increased from 16 feet to 18 feet, which allowed full extension at any angle below 45 degrees with a full payload. The tower designation was changed to the MZ-100, the first of which went to Baton Rouge, Louisiana. Uncertainty surrounds the meaning of the MZ designation, which coincidently matched the initials of the chairman of the board.

In 1981, LTI also introduced the 55-foot Water Tower to compete with Snorkel's 50-foot Tele-Squrt. The Water Tower had a 500-pound dry tip load and a 250-pound wet rating. It was a two-section, steel, telescoping boom design with A-frame outriggers. Like the Tele-Squrt, the Water Tower had a two-section, aluminum rescue ladder along the boom. Late in 1981, the product name was changed

to the Fire Stix. LTI thought the product was red hot and gave out Jolly Rancher Fire Stix candy to trade show visitors as a tie-in. As it turned out, the aerial was too heavy to properly compete with the Tele-Squrt, and in 1986, the product was sold to KME.

Also in 1981, LTI entered into an exclusive agreement with Mack Trucks to provide the company with an aerial

In 1984, the FDNY experimented with two 100-foot, MZ-100 ladder towers from LTI. This was the first break from the traditional mid-mounted Aerialscope tower ladders that accounted for the entire FDNY tower fleet. These units were mounted on American LaFrance low-profile Century Series chassis at a time when the city was buying pumpers from American LaFrance. They were equipped with pumps and 400-gallon water tanks. Tower Ladder 14 was assigned to Harlem.

product line. Introduced as the Bulldog I, this was a completely new ladder designed by Bob Vanstone to replace the Challenger Series. The Bulldog I was only available to Mack. The ladder length was 106 feet with a 200-pound tip load. It was another four-section, steel ladder with an optional waterway. The addition of a waterway extended the fly section and, in turn, the entire aerial ladder to a length of 108 feet. The Bulldog I was offered as a rear-mount, mid-mount, or TDA, and was light enough without a waterway to be mounted on a chassis with a single rear axle. This was the first aerial by LTI with a tubular design for the torque box. The Bulldog I had two rear outriggers with a 16-foot jack spread and two midship-mounted downriggers for the rear-mounted units. The stabilizers were reversed in position for a mid-mounted unit. The first Bulldog I went to Ogunquit, Maine. The LTI serial number of 813101 could be interpreted as follows: the first two digits represented the year when the order was placed, the next two digits indicated what number aerial this was overall since the beginning of that year, and the final two digits indicated the Bulldog I type. During the life span of the Bulldog I, a total of 25 units were sold.

In 1981, LTI also introduced the AS-75, a 75-foot aerial ladder. The first unit went to Jollyville, Texas, with a Van Pelt body and a serial number of 819578. It was a modified Bulldog aerial now named the Aqua Stix. The three-section aerial had a 400-pound dry tip load and a 200-pound wet rating. It was actually the Bulldog I–style ladder minus the fly section. This had a new torque box design and utilized two rear outriggers that were lower than those used on other LTI aerials. The Aqua Stix name was dropped from the product several years later.

In 1982, LTI completed the move of its production from Leola, Pennsylvania, to the facilities in Ephrata, Pennsylvania. Also in 1982, Grumman began making and marketing a platform aerial and severed its ties with LTI. The final Grumman-LTI combination was believed to be serial number 802486, which was ordered in 1980 and delivered in 1981. At the same time, LTI ventured into the airport crash truck market by introducing the Trident. This was built by Conestoga on a 4x4 Duplex chassis and incorporated a 55-foot Fire Stix aerial with full pump and roll capabilities. LTI added outriggers to accommodate structural applications as well. It became too complicated and cumbersome for the task it had been designed for and LTI never proceeded past the prototype unit.

In 1982, the Miami City and the Metro-Dade County fire departments were looking to purchase several heavy-duty aerial devices. They wanted platform aerials and straight ladders. They sponsored independent testing to verify LTI's claims as to the capabilities of the MZ-100. In response to overwhelming satisfaction with the testing results, Metro-Dade placed an order for seven aerials, two of which had platforms. To meet the balance of the order, LTI introduced the ML3S-100, an MZ-100 without the platform. Four of these units (serial numbers 8204196–8204496) were built and delivered. These had a 1,000-pound rating and maintained all of the characteristics and specifications of the ladder tower. They had an extended fly section with pinnable waterways, which had electro-hydraulic monitors capable of operating at any point. Miami's fire department purchased one MZ-100 unit.

In 1983 when Mack ceased manufacturing fire apparatus, the Bulldog I replaced the much heavier New Generation Series as the primary LTI aerial ladder. The new designation became the Quadra Stix. The QS Series, as it was generally called, offered the QS-106, which was the 106-foot rear-mount, and the QS-106 TDA, which was the 106-foot TDA. The QS series had a 250-pound tip load. When fitted with a waterway, the fly section was extended to protect the nozzle, thereby lengthening the ladder. The designation then was a QS-108 or a QS-108 TDA. For a specific customer request, the fly section could be removed to create an 85-foot ladder, although there were too few ever built to formally initiate a QS-85 model name.

In 1984, Pierce began looking to replace LTI as its exclusive source for aerials. Pierce wanted a unique product that could not be offered from other body builders and no longer wanted to compete with Conestoga Custom Products as an OEM. In turn, Pierce left LTI and began working with Smeal in 1985. Westfield, Texas, received the last combination Pierce-LTI unit with a 75-foot aerial ladder. The LTI serial number was 8302378 and the Pierce job number was E-2251.

LTI realized a need for its own identity for sales and marketing. The company unveiled the Olympian custom chassis in 1985 at the New York State Chiefs Show. It was initially incorporated with a new pumper program to expand the LTI product line into a full mix of fire apparatus. The cab had a unique modern design with a sloped front and contoured corners. Kidron, who also fabricated the modern cab for Hahn, made the Olympian cab, and Duplex supplied the chassis. The first few were assembled at LTI, with the balance of complete cab and chassis assembly being handled at Duplex in Midvale, Ohio. The first

In 1985, LTI introduced a proprietary cab and chassis design called the Olympian. One of the first units went to the Lopatcong Fire Department in Delaware Park, New York. The Olympian offered a slanted cab front and square fenders, producing a different visual look for LTI. This 1986 unit had a 75-foot Aqua Stix aerial ladder.

Olympian pumper went to Harrisonburg, Virginia, and the first Olympian chassis with an aerial was sold to Duluth, Minnesota, with serial number 8506578.

In 1986, LTI was bought by Simon, a British company that also purchased Duplex two years later. Also in 1986, LTI went to a modular bucket for the ladder towers, which in the event of an accident was much easier and less costly to replace. That same year, the fire department in Lawrence, Kansas, which is home to the University of Kansas, wanted a super heavy-duty aerial ladder capable of evacuating a large number of people. Using FMC as an OEM, the department was promised the ML3S-100, which had been designed for Dade County. At the time of delivery, however, they received an HL4S-100 that was promptly refused and returned to FMC in Orlando. LTI later agreed to build the ML3S-100 for them with a serial number of 8604096. It became a showpiece for LTI, which had claimed to have the strongest aerial ladder in America, and challenged any competitor to meet them at the IAFC in St. Louis for a test. No one accepted LTI's challenge.

When LTI introduced the QS Series in 1983, the pre-piped ladder had been classified with a length of 108 feet. Upon re-examination, it was determined that the fly extension added to protect the waterway was actually closer to 4 feet. Toward the latter part of 1986, the QS-108 was redesignated as a QS-110 to better reflect the actual ladder length.

In 1988, LTI introduced the QH-110. The first unit went to Lakewood, New York, with serial number 8806892. This was the Quadra Heavy aerial with a 500-pound tip load wet or dry. This was a totally new design with wider rung rails than the QS series. In addition, the QH had heavier lift cylinders, higher handrails, and a heavier turntable. The QH-110 was also offered with a waterway. This was available as a rear-mount or TDA. The 110-foot tractor-drawn was viewed as too long by some, so it was shortened and offered as a 100-foot QH-100. Initially, the TDAs required swing-out stabilizer jacks that extended in an arc to the set position. The spread was 18 feet and there was no option for short jacking the outriggers. Deployment required a lot of room for the jacks to swing outward and away from the trailer. In the event that there was not enough room for the outriggers, the trailer could be jack-knifed to offset the opposite side outrigger. In the mid-1990s, the swing-out design was replaced with two sets of traditional outriggers with the same 18-foot spread, allowing easier deployment and requiring less space on the fire ground for set up. Atlanta was one of the last customers for the swing-out jacks. Sixty-four QH-110 units were produced through 1996. The last unit was a tractor-drawn with a tandem axle tractor for Columbus, Ohio, and a serial number of 9604509.

In 1989, the MZ-100 ladder tower was replaced by the ST2000. This had redesigned ladder sections and used the same outriggers and torque box as the previous design, with an increased tip load of 1,000 pounds. The first ST2000, with serial number 8806521, was delivered to Gary, Indiana, and was built on an Olympian chassis with a mid-engine design.

Mack

In 1981, Mack introduced the Bulldog I line of steel aerials. This series was a private label product line produced for Mack by LTI. The Bulldog I Series offered midship ladders, rear-mounted ladders, and TDAs. These were four-section, 106-foot, steel aerials that were primarily offered on the CF611 chassis with a variety of engine options from 235 to 350 horsepower. Single- or tandem-axle models were available with the added options of a 250 gallon-per-minute booster pump, a midship-mounted pump capable of up to 2,000 gallons per minute, and a 200-gallon water tank. The first, with serial number 813101 (the "01" signified a rear-mount Bulldog I), was shipped to Ogunquit, Maine, and the second unit went to Spring Garden Township in York County, Pennsylvania, shortly thereafter. In 1982, the FDNY received two rear-mounted Bulldog I ladder trucks. The first midmount Bulldog I with serial number 816502 ("02" signified a mid-mount Bull-

Beginning in 1981, Mack contracted with LTI for an exclusive line of aerial ladders. Named the Bulldog I Series, two of these 106-foot aerials were sold to the FDNY. L132, assigned to Brooklyn, went by the name "Eye of the Storm." In the two years that the Bulldog program ran, 25 units were produced.

dog) went to Millinocket, Maine, in 1981 and the first tiller with serial number 8200103 ("03" signified a TDA Bulldog) was sold to Downey, California. The Bulldog I aerials were offered with a pre-piped waterway. These aerials came with an extended fly section to protect the nozzle, and subsequently were rated at 108 feet. Internally, LTI classified the pre-piped units as Bulldog II aerials. Four of the pre-piped units were manufactured under the Bulldog Series—one mid-mount, two rear-mounts, and one tractor-drawn unit with an MC chassis for Atlantic City, New Jersey. The last Bulldog aerial, ordered in 1983, was completed in 1984 and delivered to Andover, Massachusetts, with serial number 8302704 ("04" signified a rear-mount Bulldog II). The Bulldog program did not prove overly successful with 25 aerials being sold before Mack ceased the production of fire trucks in 1983.

From that point on, Mack continued to produce the CF Series fire chassis for other builders who mounted bodies and aerials on them, including Baker, the producer of the Aerialscope.

In 1985, a new Aerialscope was introduced with a reach of 95 feet and an 800-pound load capacity. The first of what

would be a total of 35 of these units on CF chassis went to Providence, Rhode Island, in 1986. After Mack stopped fabricating bodies, the Aerialscope was still sold in 75-foot and 95-foot models exclusively on Mack CF Series chassis. Baker was selling them with bodies built by Saulsbury until 1990 when the CF chassis was discontinued.

Maxim

In 1985, Maxim re-opened again as Maxim, Inc. under new ownership. The company offered pumpers and aerials with the cab-forward F-Series and the conventional S-Series chassis. A Canadian company purchased 50 percent of Maxim in 1987, and then purchased the other 50 percent in 1988 in order to infuse more capital into the operation. During 1989, Maxim was building about one truck per week. One of the last aerials produced was a tractor-drawn unit for Cambridge, Massachusetts. Maxim closed for the last time in December of 1989. The remaining inventory and assets were auctioned off. Aerial parts and rights were bought by a company that provided service to Maxim customers, and the remaining custom cabs were purchased by KME and offered as an option to its customers.

Pierce

In the early 1980s, Pierce had a full line of LTI aerials including the Fire Stix, New Generation aerials, and both the 85-foot and 100-foot ladder towers. Pierce was looking for autonomy with its product line and began to investigate alternative aerial suppliers to replace LTI in 1983. Pierce visited with Smeal Fire Apparatus, which had a steel aerial ladder on display at the IAFC convention that year in Atlanta.

In 1984, Pierce entered into an agreement to buy aerial ladders from Smeal in Nebraska, severing ties with LTI. Smeal had sold a relatively small number of these aerials themselves, and wanted to continue to market them in areas surrounding Nebraska. Pierce had exclusive access to the products with the exception of South Dakota, Nebraska, Kansas, and Iowa.

The available ladders included a three-section, 75-foot, steel rear-mount, and a four-section, 105-foot rear-mount. Both devices were available with or without a pre-piped waterway. A short time later, the two-section, 55-foot aerial was added to the line followed by a midship 105-foot aerial in 1987 and a 105-foot TDA in 1988. These ladders were rated at 500 pounds dry and 400 pounds wet. The 55-foot

and 75-foot aerials used two H-style outriggers for support while the 105-foot ladders required four. Jack spread for the 55-foot was 13 feet, 10 inches, and for the 75- and 105-foot units the spread was 16 feet.

The TDA had a 400-pound tip load and used two swing-out, H-style outriggers with an 18-foot spread. The original tractor featured a modified Dash cab with a raised

In 1987, the Pierce aerial line that was built by Smeal added a 105-foot mid-mount ladder. The first four-section aerial was mounted onto a Dash tilt-cab chassis and delivered to the Brookline Fire Company in Havertown, Pennsylvania. This did not prove to be a sought-after product and it was eventually discontinued.

When Pierce severed ties with LTI, the company entered into an agreement for a new ladder tower with SFI, a company started by former LTI employees. Together, under the Pierce name, they introduced the 110-foot Pierce aerial platform in 1984, which was available exclusively on the Pierce Arrow chassis. The optional fully enclosed four-door cab was specified on this 1988 tower quint for New City, New York.

roof panel that allowed the tillerman to see the cab over the ladder. Pierce also had a turntable leveling system capable of adjusting to a 10-degree front-to-back angle and 4 degrees from side to side.

Pierce needed a platform aerial when it stopped selling the LTI units. In 1984, Pierce began designing a platform aerial with the help of a small company in Pennsylvania formed by a former LTI employee named Ken Merica. Structural Fabrications, Inc. (SFI), designed a 1,000-pound, 95-foot three-section, and an 800-pound, 110-foot, three-section platform aerial. These aerials used the industry standard four H-style outriggers. Unlike other platforms, the Pierce bucket was introduced with open sides. Pierce purchased SFI in 1988 and kept production there for a few years before moving it to Kewaunee Engineering in Kewaunee, Wisconsin. This same facility would later also build the straight aerial ladder sections. The first 110-foot aerial platform, job number E2301, went to Morehead, Kentucky. Between 1984 and 1986, Pierce manufactured a total of nine 110-foot aerial platforms.

In late 1986, Pierce redesigned the aerial platform and began to market a 105-foot aerial platform with an 800-pound tip load. Unlike the 110-foot model, this unit had a platform with solid sides. The first 105-foot aerial platform was sent to Waterloo, Iowa, after being showcased at the IAFC convention that year in Dallas. The 105-foot aerial platform was in production until 1989, with all units being produced at the SFI facility.

Pirsch

In 1983, Pirsch unveiled a new aerial ladder design. The Skytop, as it was called, was a four-section, 110-foot aluminum ladder with a 200-pound tip load. This new design incorporated several changes from the earlier ladder, which was still available after the release of the Skytop. Changes included a pre-piped waterway option along the entire ladder, "K" bracing, hydraulic cylinders pulling the extension cables, and nylatron pads replacing rollers between the ladder sections. The Skytop also used four H-style stabilizers. The construction differed from the previous design in the use of welded bottom rails and ladder rungs that were made of hollow, tubular aluminum extrusions instead of the "T" rails. The uprights and top rails

were still riveted. Pirsch wanted to retain the use of rivets because of their long-standing use in Pirsch ladders. These changes enabled Pirsch to increase the capacity and add 10 feet in length. Although the Skytop and the earlier Pirsch ladder designs shared the 200-pound rating, the stability and use of the new ladder was greater than the original design. The Skytop had greater maneuverability and was rated to operate at low angles, unlike the previous design. This distinction of a greater range of operation was particularly important for Pirsch's ability to compete with other aerial builders and keep up with the demands of the fire service. The original aerial ladder designs, like so many others that originated in the 1930s, were meant to be no more than long, powered ground ladders. These were intended to increase the height that could be reached with a ladder raised by men and have the ability to turn for better positioning. Aerial ladder designs were meant to have the tip supported by resting against a building during ladder operations. The ladders were not built for cantilevered support. When the fire service wanted to add

Pierce and Smeal added a tractor-drawn aerial in 1988. The TDA had a 400-pound tip load and used two swing-out, H-style outriggers with an 18-foot spread. The original tractor featured a modified Dash cab with a raised roof panel that allowed the tillerman to see the cab. The first customer for the Pierce TDA was the Pittsburgh Fire Department.

water tower abilities to aerial ladders, more manpower on the ladders, and to perform rescues without having to be supported by a building, these early designs were not able to handle the tasks.

The Skytop could be ordered on a single- or tandem-axle chassis. Roughly nine of these units were sold to loyal Pirsch customers before the first demo unit was built. The demo unit, built on a single-axle chassis, was displayed and demonstrated at the Baltimore Fire Expo in 1984 and the Fire Expo in Lancaster County, Pennsylvania. It was later sold to the Cleveland Heights Fire Department in Ohio. The first unit that was built specifically for a customer was a tandem-axle unit purchased by the Gates, New York, Fire District. The ladder would extend over the front of the cab on a single-axle chassis while a tandem axle would align the ladder with the front of the cab. For no apparent reason, other than that it was easier to manufacture, Pirsch aerials were squared off at the end instead of having a tapered fly section like many of Pirsch's competitors.

When departments began to request quints and add high side compartments on both sides that would be full of equipment, the weight considerations required a tandem-axle chassis. The aluminum body and aluminum aerial ladder were all relatively lightweight, and therefore viable on a single-axle chassis. Bodies were available in aluminum or galvaneal steel. Marion Body Works, also in Wisconsin, built the first aluminum aerial body for the Skytop demo. After that, Pirsch built the aluminum aerial bodies, although another manufacturer, Ranger, built several aluminum bodies for Pirsch pumpers.

The Skytop was offered as a rear-mount or a TDA. Only three 110-foot Skytop TDAs were ever built. One went to Little Rock, Arkansas, one was delivered to a department in Tennessee, and the third was one of two TDAs ever sold to the United States Navy.

One Skytop was produced as a 75-foot quint. This was achieved by removing one of the ladder sections from the 110-foot model. Only one of these units was ever built. Another one-of-a-kind aerial was built and sold to the Bryn Mawr Fire Company in Pennsylvania. It was the only Pirsch aerial to be mounted on a custom fire truck chassis built by a competitor who offered their own aerial. A 110-foot Skytop aerial with Pirsch bodywork was mounted on a Hahn custom chassis at the fire department's request.

Pirsch sales and engineering proposed building a 135-foot ladder to compete with Emergency One, in addition to a heavier 110-foot ladder. Both would have required a new base section and some other changes to the Skytop design. A lack of finances stopped these projects and Pirsch went out of business in 1985.

In 1983, Pirsch unveiled a new aerial ladder design. The Skytop, as it was called, was a four-section, 110-foot, aluminum ladder with a 200-pound tip load. This new design incorporated several changes from the earlier ladder. While the demo unit was a quint on a single-axle chassis, some customers requested units with tandem axles. That year also marked the changeover from the 86-inch Cincinnati Cab to the wider, 94-inch cab.

Seagrave

In the 1980s, Seagrave continued to build the Rear Admiral. This was a 100-foot, four-section, rear-mounted aerial ladder on a single-axle chassis. The aerial required two rear-mounted, A-type stabilizers with a 150-inch spread. It offered a low-profile cab for a lower travel height and had an option for a Rear Admiral quint with a water tank and Waterous pump. The Rear Admiral was modified in the early 1980s to offer a heavier duty ladder with a 200-pound tip load. This aerial required a tandem-axle chassis and had two rear-mounted, H-style outriggers. It was available as a TDA, which required replacing the standard A-style jacks with two swing-out jacks under the turntable.

In 1984, Seagrave added a 75-foot aerial to the Rear Admiral Series. This was a three-section steel ladder that shared the single-axle design with the 100-foot Rear Admiral, but used H-style outriggers with a 17-foot spread like the heavy-duty ladder. This aerial also required a single downrigger under the truck's cab. Aerial controls were located at the pump panel instead of having a control station on the turntable. The 75-foot Rear Admiral was offered on a 92-inch-wide, low-profile custom Seagrave chassis with a 300-gallon water tank and a choice of Waterous pumps.

In 1985, Seagrave re-introduced a line of more economical aerials on a commercial chassis. Offered with a Ford C-8000 Series chassis, the Invincible Series aerial featured a four-section, 100-foot, rear-mounted steel aerial with a steel body. The 150-inch jack spread and two A-style rear outriggers were common to the 100-foot Rear Admiral. Roughly 28 of these units were produced before being discontinued in 1991.

In 1987, Seagrave released the RA110. This was a new heavy-duty addition to the aerial products. Stronger and longer, this 110-foot aerial ladder was marketed with a 550-pound rating. Prior to this time, Seagrave only offered a ladder with weight ratings of 200 pounds. The RA110 required a tandem axle. This new aerial utilized four H-style outriggers with a 17-foot spread. It was offered in galvaneal or stainless steel with a 94-inch-wide standard custom cab or Seagrave's low-profile cab to lower the travel height. The first RA110 was sold to the Northlake, Illinois, fire department with a low-profile cab.

The Chicago Fire Department purchased many Rear Admiral ladders from Seagrave, including Truck 47 pictured here. In order to utilize these aerials for elevated master stream operations at a fire scene, it was necessary to mount the nozzle at the tip, drag the hose to the nozzle, and secure the line to several ladder rungs for safety. Ropes were used to control the nozzle from the ground, rather than sending a firefighter to the tip of the ladder.

Seagrave was able to increase the tip load rating for the Rear Admiral TDA by replacing the midship A-style jacks with longer swing-out style jacks for greater stability. This 1984 unit for Cleveland, Ohio, also shows a stiffer base section closest to the turntable.

Smeal

After building its first aerial ladder back in 1963, Smeal built its next unit, a 75-foot ladder, in 1972 for a fire department in Seward, Nebraska. In 1981, Smeal built a three-section, 85-foot aerial for Vermillion, South Dakota, and then a 65-foot platform aerial for Falls City, Nebraska, later in the same year. The platform was a three-section, rear-mounted unit with a 750-pound capacity that used four H-style outriggers with a 16-foot spread. Another, similar platform aerial went to Summerville, South Carolina, the following year. The platforms were built on International and Mack chassis respectively.

By 1983, Smeal had sold roughly 20 aerial devices. They had a booth at the IAFC trade show in Atlanta that year to display a 75-foot aerial, where Doug Ogilvie of

Pierce Manufacturing approached Don Smeal. He wanted to discuss an agreement by which Pierce would purchase aerial ladders exclusively from Smeal, ending Pierce's relationship with LTI.

Between 1984 and 1992, Smeal was the sole provider of aerial ladders marketed by Pierce. Smeal also retained the rights to market ladders under the Smeal name in a select distribution area surrounding the factory in Nebraska and in 1984, Smeal built a four-section, 104-foot aerial for Prestonsburg, Kentucky. This had a tip load of 400 pounds and utilized four H-style outriggers.

Snorkel

As early as 1981, Emergency One was an OEM with Snorkel and in 1985, Grumman joined the ranks. At that

78

time, Pierce was a principal distributor of Snorkels and Tele-Squrts. Pierce and Grumman used Waterous pumps exclusively, while Emergency One was a Hale customer. Fire departments with a specific pump requirement that wanted a Snorkel product had to find an OEM that could provide their preferred brand of pump. If the departments needed a Waterous pump, they had to go to Pierce or Grumman; for a Hale pump, they would need to contact Emergency One or Seagrave.

By the mid-1980s, Snorkel's fire division accounted for less than 5 percent of its total sales, due in large part to the emergence of the telescoping ladder towers. However, by the late 1980s, Snorkel had become the largest U.S. manufacturer of self-propelled work platforms for the construction trade, which offset the decreasing fire sales.

On a historical note, Snorkel repurchased the original 50-foot Pitman Snorkel in 1987 and completely restored it. The unit was subsequently sent to the American LaFrance museum in Cleveland, North Carolina.

In 1988, Snorkel introduced the Tele-Squrt 65. This was a three-section combination aerial and telescopic water tower. It could be mounted on a single-axle chassis and had a rated tip load of 250 or 500 pounds, distributed at any angle from 10 degrees below to 85 degrees above horizontal, while flowing water. The dry rating at zero degrees was 500 pounds and increased to 800 pounds above 45 degrees. Jack spread was 11 feet, 4 inches.

Steeldraulics

In 1980, an engineer left LTI and started a company called Steeldraulics in Shafferstown, Pennsylvania. He started to work on designing an aerial to compete with LTI when firefighters from Elizabethtown, Pennsylvania, a local

In 1987, Seagrave introduced the RA110. This was a new heavy-duty aerial that was both stronger and longer than the Rear Admiral, with a 110-foot length and a 550-pound rating. Prior to this time, Seagrave offered only a ladder with weight ratings of up to 200 pounds. This new aerial utilized four H-style outriggers with a 17-foot spread. The demo was built with a low-profile cab and was sold to the Northlake, Illinois, Fire Department.

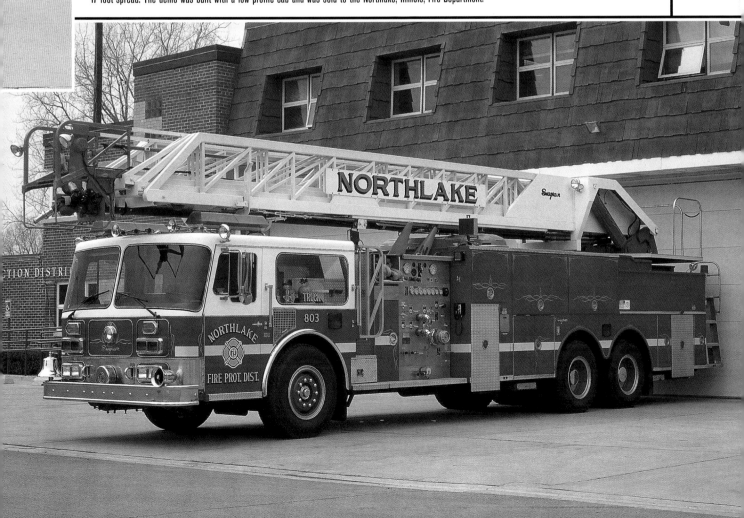

fire company, heard about the new company and visited the small facility. They were interested in buying this new aerial and were referred to Grumman Emergency Products. Grumman had been looking for a replacement supplier for LTI and had made arrangements with Steeldraulics to try the aerial. The first unit was completed in 1982.

In 1983, Steeldraulics moved to Lancaster, Pennsylvania, and produced five more units for Grumman, who then purchased the designs and took over fabrication in the Lancaster facility, eventually moving production to Roanoke, Virginia.

Steeldraulics then worked as a company that primarily refurbished fire apparatus. The company also built four steel aerial ladders under the Steeldraulics name. These ladders were sold to the San Francisco Fire Department. Two units were 75-foot quints and two were 100-foot TDAs. Controversy between the fire department, the firefighter's union, and the city resulted in the 75-foot quints being sold by the city and never going into service. The TDAs were assigned to city ladder companies.

In 1986, Steeldraulics again entered the aerial market with an agreement to design and build several devices for FMC. After building one 102-foot, rear-mounted ladder that was sold to the Wayne Township Fire Department in Indiana, the relationship between Steeldraulics and FMC was abandoned. Steeldraulics went out of business in 1987.

Steeldraulics emerged as a new company shortly thereafter, under the name of Firefab and it was contracted to build a family of aerials in the early 1990s for Firewolf, another new company. Firefab produced only three tower ladders in 1993 before Firewolf was shutdown in 1996.

Sutphen

In 1981, Sutphen stunned much of the fire industry when it sold the FDNY two 100 + aerial tower quints. This was the first FDNY purchase of tower ladders that were not Aerialscope devices by Baker. Of the two units, one saw service in Harlem as TL14 and the other in Brooklyn as TL119. These were the tallest tower ladders in the FDNY fleet and saw quite a bit of fire duty with two very busy companies.

In 1981, Sutphen built a 65-foot ladder on a single-axle chassis. Similar in box-type, lattice braced construction to the aerial towers, this new product was a straight ladder with a pre-piped waterway. The ladder's box design offered a protected area for the waterway to travel to the tip without the possibility of damage, unlike competitors' units with the waterways running underneath the ladder. This ladder was called

the Fireball and had an 800-pound tip load rating. This new aerial was offered on a Sutphen custom chassis with an 86-inch-wide cab and open, rear facing jump seats on a single-axle chassis. Like Sutphen's towers, these were also quints with 1,500 gallon-per-minute Hale pumps and 500-gallon water tanks. Two midship-mounted, A-style jacks provided stabilization for aerial operations. Like a pumper, this new quint featured high side compartments for additional equipment storage. High handrails were incorporated into the top of the box boom construction for ease of climbing. Body construction was standard with three high compartments on the driver's side above two lower compartments, one on either side of the wheelwell. In 1984, the company added a three-section, 75-foot model sharing all of the other features and characteristics of the three-section, 65-foot aerial.

In 1982, Sutphen began to offer the newer, 94-inch-wide Cincinnati Cab as an option, though some departments were still ordering the 86-inch model. It wasn't until several years later that Sutphen had a call for fully enclosed four-door cabs.

Sutphen introduced a five-section, 100-foot tower in 1984. Except for the additional ladder section, the rest of the specifications were the same as for the 90-foot, 100 + tower. Less than 10 of these units were sold in the roughly two-year period that it was offered.

In 1985, a three-section, 65-foot, twin platform design was introduced with one platform on each side of the ladder. The dual platforms had a 750-pound capacity. Due to the added weight of the aerial, the water tank capacity was reduced to 400 gallons. This style was available until 1991 when the last unit was sold to Newcomerstown, Ohio.

In 1987, Pemfab, one of the four independent makers of custom fire truck chassis, was offering private label agreements to provide a proprietary tilt-cab to apparatus builders. Sutphen did not take advantage of the private labeling but did purchase several chassis from Pemfab for customer orders. At the time, Sutphen only offered a fixed cab and chassis. Pemfab provided a 94-inch-wide Cincinnati Cab with the engine moved forward for a larger crew seating area. The engine rested between the driver and officer. This eliminated the bench seat, which could accommodate an additional firefighter in the front; but offered a full-width rear facing jump seat area without the intrusion of the engine house. This new tilt-cab had a wide, brushed stainless steel panel that ran from the outside of the headlight stanchions on either side and had a grill pattern cut into the center third. Pemfab also was able to offer chassis with a quicker turnaround time than Sutphen could produce in its

This unit was built in 1987 for Warren, Michigan. It is slightly unique, considering that it was mounted on a Pemfab chassis instead of the standard custom Sutphen chassis. Pemfab at the time was marketing private label configurations to various companies, but Sutphen opted simply for the standard Imperial cab. Pemfab supplied roughly six chassis to Sutphen. This was a quint with a 65-foot aerial and a bucket mounted on either side of the ladder.

own plant. Most of the Pemfab chassis were for pumpers, but a few were for aerials.

In 1989, the 90-foot aerial tower was modified to create a 95-foot model. It shared all of the features and characteristics of the 100 + aerial platform. This unit had a 1,000-pound tip load and an 18-foot spread with the two midship outriggers. Extending the hydraulic cylinders and shortening the overlap of the ladder sections accomplished the added length. The 100 + designation was then dropped in favor of the 90-foot and 95-foot labels.

Also in 1989, Sutphen reintroduced a true 100-foot tower. Unlike the earlier five-section unit, this was a four-section aerial with larger ladder sections and heavier aluminum beams. Other specifications matched the 90- and 95-foot towers.

At the same time, fire departments began to request fully enclosed cabs in conjunction with the National Fire Protection Association (NFPA) regulation 1901. Sutphen had a concern here that did not affect most other builders. The location of the midship turntable and the shape at the base of the aerial housing in relation to the back of the cab prevented them from utilizing an industry standard enclosed cab with a straight vertical back wall. Sutphen had to engineer its cabs with a rear wall that sloped slightly toward the front, allowing additional clearance for the aerial base. This feature was achieved by adapting front cab doors that already featured a slope along the "A" pillar to be mounted backwards for the rear of the cab. These rear doors were hinged along the straight edge over the wheelwell. This unique design made the Sutphen cab stand out from the others. Until now, body and compartment configuration had almost no variations. Beginning at this time, departments were able to reconfigure ground-ladder placement with the option for increased storage capacity with high side compartments.

Aerial Innovations

In 1993, Aerial Innovations (AI) began manufacturing aerial devices for the fire service. AI was started by a group of former LTI employees who left that company when it was purchased by Simon. AI made aerials to be marketed in conjunction with a group of OEMs that did not have an aerial line to offer. Each product received a three-digit model designation. The first was a letter representing the model's chronological place in the evolution of the AI product line. The first product was the "A" ladder, a 75-foot heavy-duty aerial. The second digit represented the number of ladder sections, and the final letter denoted whether the aerial was rear-mounted, midship, or tractor-drawn. The three-section, heavy-duty, 75-foot rear-mount (A3R) was the premier unit in 1993 with the first unit sold by Quality to Milton, Delaware. This had a 500-pound rating, wet or dry.

In 1994, the "B" unit was designed. It was a B4R, a metric ladder developed for the overseas market that never went into production. Also in 1994, the A3M was introduced along with the D-Series aerials. The D4M, D4R, and D4T were four-section, heavy-duty, 105-foot mid-mount, rear-mount, and TDA models with 500-pound ratings, wet or dry. These utilized four H-style jacks with a 16-foot spread. The first 105-foot aerial was a D4T with bodywork by RD Murray for District Heights, Maryland.

The "C" aerial was designed in 1994 but not introduced until 1995. This was a light-duty, 105-foot aerial with a 250-pound dry rating that was offered as a C4R and a C4T. These utilized two downriggers and two rear H-style outriggers with a 16-foot spread. In essence, the C-Series was the same ladder as the D-Series with less stability because of the difference in the jack design.

An E-ONE 95-foot platform aerial in the foreground is operating at an extra alarm fire in Chicago. Even though the bucket is not visible in the photo, the aerial type can be determined by counting the number of ladder sections. Three represents a platform, while four or five would be a straight ladder. The trash dumpsters did not present a problem for spotting the aerial because the jack spread with the underslung, crisscross jack system is narrow. In the background, six additional master streams are at work including one from an E-ONE ladder and another from an LTI tower.

An E-ONE HM100 ladder is being used as an elevated master stream at a structure fire. The pump operator is able to stand on a pullout shelf, giving him better access to the controls since the aerial has been lifted off the ground by the jacks. The remote controlled nozzle is being manipulated at the turntable, saving a firefighter from having to climb to the tip of the ladder. The 1994 quint is owned by the Northfield Fire Department in Illinois.

market, could be modified or re-packaged, tested, and offered to customers in roughly six months. The CR100 was offered with an extended fly section when ordered with a pre-piped waterway. Originally, it was offered on a Hurricane tilt-cab chassis only, but it became available on the Cyclone II chassis in 1999. The Milwaukee Fire Department put several CR100 aerials into service.

In 1995, the HP75 was also introduced. This ladder had a two-person tip capacity with a 500-pound rating. It utilized H-style outriggers, a single rear axle chassis, a 500-gallon water tank, and the same substructure as the HP70 with a 16-foot jack spread. This aerial was offered on the

mid-engine Hush, the Hurricane fixed, tilt, or mid-engine chassis, the Cyclone tilt-cab, and then the newer Cyclone II chassis. This was a new ladder design. It featured diamond extrusions instead of the rectangular "C" channel style utilized on the older family of aerials. The weight of the ladder sections was the same as the other 75-foot aerial offered by E-ONE, but the new design allowed them to double the tip load. This was a more difficult ladder to manufacture. The fly section of the HP75 was extended to accommodate a water monitor with a pre-piped waterway. Previous aerials had to extend each ladder section when a waterway was added instead of just the tip or fly section.

In 1996, E-ONE introduced the new Cyclone II cab with a comprehensive redesign of the entire cab to include more headroom, a lower doghouse, and other upgrades. Seven sizes were initially offered with rear-of-cab-to-axle dimensions ranging from 44 to 80 inches, and three different raised roof options with new, tall doors.

E-ONE added another product to the line of diamond-extruded aerials in 1996. The HP100 optimized the 100-foot ladder with a 500-pound tip load (plus a 50-pound equipment allowance). This was intended to replace the CR100 until customer requests for the 800-pound ladder convinced E-ONE that the CR100 should remain in the line. The HP100 required a tandem-axle chassis and had a 12-foot jack spread. It utilized the integral torque box chassis with four underslung crisscross scissors jacks. These jacks allowed for more compartment space with less intrusion into the body than H-style jacks. The HP100 was designed to carry as much as 500 gallons of water, and for mounting on the Cyclone II chassis, although it could be fitted on a Hurricane at the customer's request.

Also in 1996, Federal Signal Corporation, E-ONE's parent company, purchased Bronto, a maker of fire and industrial aerial devices from Finland. Previously, Bronto had been marketed in the United States through an agreement with Pierce. E-ONE designers spent much of 1997 engineering and mounting a 135-foot Bronto Skylift onto an E-ONE torque box. Subsequently, the first several ladders built in Finland were shipped to the United States and then mounted onto Cyclone II or Hurricane chassis, depending

on the specific aerial devices. These units used a model number beginning with the letter "F," which signified fire service booms. Bronto also manufactured aerial work platforms for the industrial market, which carried an "S" designation preceding the model number. The fire series offered units that could extend to 91 feet, 118 feet, 135 feet, and 174 feet. The first unit delivered by E-ONE was an F135 HDT delivered to Knoxville, Tennessee. The product line started with the F91 HDA. This was a 91-foot, heavy duty articulating, three-boom aerial. When bedded, the basket hung over the rear of the vehicle. The F91 HDA had a 1,000-pound tip load dry, 750 pounds wet, or 500 pounds wet with dual nozzles in the platform. The platform was built to accommodate an additional 243 pounds of permanently mounted equipment. Jack spread for the F91 HDA was 16 feet, 4 inches. The next aerials in the product line were part of the HDT, or Heavy Duty Telescoping, Series. Each of these units was rated the same as the F91 HDA. The jack spread for the HDT units was 20 feet; 17 feet, 6 inches; and 20 feet, respectively. Larger units with higher reach that were available overseas were not offered in the United

Firefighters from the Libertyville Fire Department in Lake County, Illinois, prepare to put an elevated master stream into operation using their 1992 E-ONE 75-foot aerial. The unit features a mid-engine Hush chassis. The ladder is being raised and moved toward the fire as firefighters make the hydrant with the supply line that is attached to the intake through the face of the cab. Several pre-connected hand lines have also been pulled off by the pump panel.

States, due to their size and heavy road weight. The F91 HDA, the F118 HDT, and the F135 HDT all share the same standard travel height of 12 feet, 5 inches. The first F135 HDT on an E-ONE chassis with an E-ONE torque box was purchased by Muscatine, Iowa. The second F135 HDT went to the Dallas Ft. Worth International Airport. The first F91 HDA unit went overseas to Aruba, and Saudi Arabia bought more than 30 units. The first domestic F91 HDA went to Wildwood Crest, New Jersey. Customers for the F118 HDT included Tulsa, Phoenix, Anaheim, Dubuque, and Penn Township in Pennsylvania.

The first F174 HDT, which required tandem front steering axles, was built as a demonstrator on a Hurricane chassis with no crew section. While it was in south Florida at a demonstration and open house for the local dealer in 1999, there was a fire in Miami at the American Airlines sports arena, which was under construction. The fire involved plywood forms and construction equipment in the upper tier section at a location that was over 160 feet off the ground and out of reach for the fire department. The fire department had been on-scene for roughly three hours with firefighters attempting to climb the construction scaffold with 2 1/2-inch attack lines, when the F174 HDT was driven to Miami to offer assistance. It was promptly put into service with a 4-inch supply line from a pumper. E-ONE and Miami personnel ascended to a point above the fire and were able to extinguish it in a matter of minutes using a master stream of 450 gallons per minute.

In 1998, E-ONE began to order the Bronto torque box and outriggers with each aerial for mounting onto the E-ONE chassis. Although the outriggers were higher than the E-ONE stabilizers, the Bronto torque box was able to lower the overall height of the units. The first unit with a Bronto

torque box and an E-ONE chassis was one of the two units built for the Tulsa Oklahoma Fire Department.

Another Bronto model was the F167 HLA. The High Level Articulating boom product also required the tandem front axle chassis. The HLA unit combined telescoping booms and articulating booms together, plus a separate third boom jib. Both of the main booms articulated and telescoped. As of this writing, two of these units had been shipped by E-ONE. Both were built on Hurricane chassis— one purchased by the fire department in Calgary, Alberta,

Firefighters from Addison, Illinois, demonstrate the ability of their 1993 E-ONE HP105 platform aerial to operate safely, even if the unit is not completely level from front to back. The truck has four H-style outriggers and two underbody down-riggers for stability. With the exception of the HP105, the HP 75, and the Teleboom, all of the other E-ONE aerials utilize the underslung, crisscross jack system.

Canada, and the other by the Ciba Chemical Company for use at its Alabama plant. The F167 HLA and the F174 HDT were the tallest F-Series Bronto Skylift units available on traditional fire service chassis. If the opportunity presented itself to sell one of the taller F233 HLA or F288 HLA units through E-ONE, the aerial would be built on a five-axle Tor, Volvo, or Mercedes Benz truck chassis.

Also in 1998, the 95-foot platform aerial that was originally offered on the Hurricane and mid-engine Hush chassis was offered on the Hurricane tilt-cab chassis and the roomier Cyclone II chassis. Use with the Cyclone II resulted in a higher travel height of 12 feet, 2 inches, compared to 11 feet, 9 inches with the Hurricane.

E-ONE entered the TDA market in 1998. This product utilized an HP100 ladder mounted on a tiller chassis. E-ONE had to engineer and adapt the Cyclone II chassis to accommodate a fifth wheel assembly to pull the trailer. The tiller utilized only two jacks mounted at the base of the turntable behind the tractor. It had a spread of 17 feet, 6 inches and a 500-pound tip load, wet or dry. Five tillers were purchased by the fire department in Kansas City, Missouri, as part of an order for an excess of 30 total units. The next tiller customer was the San Bruno Fire Department in California. It purchased a tiller in 2001 along with a matching pumper. Most recently the third tiller customer became the fire department in Baltimore County, Maryland, in 2002.

In May of 1999, E-ONE entered into a marketing agreement with Spartan Motors to purchase the Advantage Series chassis, which would be sold with E-ONE pumper bodies. E-ONE referred to these chassis as its super commercial series. The Advantage chassis offered a simple cab with a flat, chrome grille, a medium four-door configuration, and no side window between the driver and crew cab doors. In the following year, the super commercial chassis were offered with the American Eagle Series 75-foot aerial. This was the first non–E-ONE custom fire service chassis in 13 years that was offered with an E-ONE aerial other than the Teleboom. Also in 1999, E-ONE discontinued the 135-foot aerial.

Ferrara

Ferrara Fire Apparatus entered the fire apparatus assembly business early in 1988 and began fabricating apparatus later the same year. In the early years the company put out 20–25 units per year. Within five years, Ferrara was turning out over 100 units annually, continually growing to exceed 200 units in the late 1990s. Ferrara entered the aerial products market with an OEM licensing agreement to sell units built by R.K. Aerials in 1992. These were mounted on commercial or custom fire truck chassis with pumps, tanks, and bodies added by Ferrara. Bodies were offered in galvaneal steel, stainless steel, or aluminum. The custom chassis generally bore the Intruder nameplate, which represented another marketing agreement between Ferrara and Spartan that was later changed to include HME for a proprietary chassis trim package. Ferrara offered 60-foot, 75-foot, and 109-foot rear-mounted, steel aerial ladders.

In 1998, Ferrara introduced a custom chassis design called the Inferno. From that point forward, many of the aerials featured the new Inferno chassis, although the HME Intruder model was still a popular choice. The R.K. Aerials products are outlined in detail under that name later in this chapter.

In August of 1999, at the FRI convention in Kansas City, Ferrara changed its aerial product supplier from R.K. Aerials to Smeal. Ferrara's products also changed. The aerial product line then consisted of 500-pound, 55-, 75-, and 105-foot, heavy-duty rear-mounted ladders, and a 100-foot, heavy-duty, mid-mounted ladder. Ferrara also offered 85-foot and 100-foot, rear-mounted aerial platforms, as well as an 85-foot, mid-mounted platform. The rear-mounted ladders were two-, three-, and four-section units. Only the 105-foot model required a tandem-axle chassis. Each featured a pre-piped waterway that had a pinnable option. The jack spreads were 13 feet, 6 inches for the 55-foot model and 18 feet for the 75-foot and 105-foot models. Two H-style outriggers were used for the 55-foot and 75-foot, while the 105-foot model used four. The 75-foot aerial had an option for two downriggers located immediately behind the cab. The 55-foot model did not have turntable controls, but they were standard for the larger models. The mid-mount aerial ladder had an overall travel height of 10 feet, 5 inches, and an 18-foot jack spread with four H-style outriggers. The tip load for the mid-mount was the same as for the other aerials.

The Ferrara aerial platforms shared the same tip load capacities as the aerial ladders. All three utilized four H-style outriggers and had an 18-foot jack spread. The bucket offered 21 square feet of space and came standard with one monitor nozzle with a capacity of up to 2,000 gallons per minute. Dual monitors were an option and all three required a tandem-axle chassis. The platforms had a 500-pound tip load capacity while flowing 1,250 gallons of water per minute or 1,000 pounds dry.

Ferrara added a low-profile version of the Inferno cab for aerials, which allowed low clearance for mid- and rear-mounted units.

Firewolf

In 1992, a group of German investors backed a pair of entrepreneurs who wanted to blend European and American technology to produce a unique line of fire apparatus in the United States. Beginning in a facility formerly owned by Piper Aircraft at the airport in Lakeland, Florida, Firewolf was formed with the intent of easing its way into production of a complete line of fire apparatus including brush trucks, commercial and custom pumpers, tankers, rescues, and aerials for the domestic and international markets. Firewolf had completed the necessary engineering for a full product line, but decided to start slowly since it was a small company. In a three-year period, Firewolf produced about a dozen units, including one airport rescue and fire fighting (ARFF) unit on a Spartan chassis, one rescue unit with a rear-mounted crane similar to units used in Europe, four

pumper tankers that were shipped to South America, two pumpers that were sold in West Virginia and Florida, and three ladder towers, two of which were sold in Mexico and the third to the Goodwill Fire Company No. 1 of York Township, Pennsylvania.

Firefab in Chambersburg, Pennsylvania, manufactured the ladder tower aerial devices. The Mexican units were built on Pemfab chassis and the York Township unit was on a Spartan chassis. Called the Skywolf, the aerial had a four-section, 105-foot steel ladder. It was stabilized by four H-style outriggers with an 18-foot spread and was constructed with two monitor nozzles in the platform. Firewolf fabricated the aerial bodies to include a 1,500 gallon-per-minute pump and a 300-gallon water tank.

In 1996, the financial backers decided to close the operation. The assets, facility, inventory, and backlog were sold to Kovatch Mobile Equipment (KME). Initially, the facility was to be added as a Florida location for KME, but after roughly eight months, the facility was closed and all remaining operations were moved to Nesquehoning, Pennsylvania. At the time of the closure, Firewolf had recently obtained orders for four straight aerial ladders going to the Czech Republic. Those orders were subsequently cancelled.

HME

HME began to supply Grumman Emergency Products with an exclusive custom cab and chassis for fire apparatus in 1989. Roughly 300 of these Panther chassis were produced before Grumman left the fire industry in 1992. Prior to that, HME had supplied chassis for the American LaFrance Century 2000 Series units beginning in 1987. After Grumman closed, HME emerged as an independent supplier of fire apparatus chassis, offering the 1871 Series for the entire fire service industry. The 1871 was already in widespread use under the Panther label with Grumman AerialCats and pumpers. All 1871 chassis featured tilt-cabs and were offered in a low-profile or standard-height version with several cab length and door options. HME entered into a licensing agreement to supply cabs and chassis under the

The Goodwill Fire Company Number 1 of York Township, Pennsylvania, received one of the three Skywolf platform aerials built by Firewolf. The other two units were shipped to Mexico. The aerial itself was built by Firefab in Chambersburg, Pennsylvania. Unlike most aerial platforms, the Skywolf had four sections and no overhang over the front of the cab.

KME adopted the stringent proof load testing procedures that had been instituted at Grumman to verify the integrity of each AerialCat produced. This involved the use of weights ranging from 2,250 pounds to 4,877

Intruder name as a proprietary model for the Ferrara pumper and aerial program in 1994. HME became the only independent custom chassis supplier to the fire service in 1997 when Spartan Motors purchased Luverne and Quality.

Kovatch Mobile Equipment (KME)

KME expanded into aerials manufacture in 1992 after purchasing the assets of Grumman Emergency Products. The AerialCat line of ladders and platforms stayed in Roanoke at what had been the Grumman facility. KME continued to capitalize on the closing of other fire apparatus companies by purchasing the assets of Firewolf in 1994.

The aerial line that KME acquired from Grumman consisted of platforms and ladders. The platform line included the 95-foot and 102-foot, AerialCat, rear-mount aerial platforms, as well as the 92-foot mid-mount platform. The ladder line consisted of the 95-foot, 100-foot, and 121-foot rear-mount ladders. Both the 95-foot and the 100-foot ladders were three-section AerialCat platforms with the buckets removed. The 121-foot was the 100-foot ladder with another fly section added.

pounds, depending on the rated capacities of each particular aerial. The weight was distributed along the fully extended ladder at an angle of zero degrees. This testing reduced the rate of weld fatigue and subjected the aerial to loads and stresses greater than what should ever be encountered in the field.

KME also had the 55-foot and 75-foot Fire Stix units prior to the Grumman purchase. Both units were two-section, telescoping water towers with aluminum rescue ladders. The tip loads were 500 pounds dry and 250 pounds wet for both models.

In 1993, KME redesigned the hydraulics and the bodies of the AerialCat line and provided the necessary engineering to mount the aerials on KME custom chassis. In 1994, KME engineers wanted a 750-pound capacity, 100-foot ladder. KME shortened the four sections of the 121-foot ladder and lowered the handrails, while keeping the same four jacks and 18-foot spread. This unit was shorter than the three-section, 100-foot ladder with the 1,000-pound rating and more marketable. The wet rating was 500 pounds. Both 100-foot ladders used the same four H-style outriggers with an 18-foot spread.

Also in 1993, KME developed a three-section, 75-foot, rear-mount aerial. This was a new design based on the original ladders with the force distribution members and a similar torque box. The 75-foot had a 14-foot spread with two rear H-style outriggers, plus two downriggers located just behind the cab. When mounted on a single-axle chassis, the unit had a 500-pound rating, wet or dry. The 75-foot could also be mounted on a tandem-axle chassis with everything else remaining the same and achieve an increased dry rating of 750 pounds. The first 750-pound, 75-foot aerial was delivered to Crossville, Tennessee, in 1994.

In 1995, KME introduced a mid-mount version of the four-section, 100-foot ladder. This had the same four outriggers and 18-foot spread as the rear-mount, but offered a travel height of 9 feet, 7 inches. The tip load was 750 pounds dry and 500 pounds wet.

In 1995, without having produced any of the four-section, 92-foot, mid-mount aerial platforms designed by Grumman, KME lengthened the sections of this aerial to achieve a length of 95 feet. The 18-foot spread of the 92-foot unit was the same for the 95-foot model. The first unit went to Conyers, New York, in 1996. Unlike the Grumman

This is a 102-foot KME AerialCat platform aerial built in 1996 for Elgin, Illinois, on a Renegade chassis. The cab roof is notched to lower the travel height, while still allowing the maximum headroom for firefighters in the rear. It is equipped with a 2,000 gallon-per-minute pump and a 150-gallon water tank. Air horns and an electronic siren are mounted behind the bumper for noise reduction but the large mechanical siren does not fit anywhere except right out in the open. An additional set of revolving warning lights is mounted on the bumper as a means of emphasizing the warning that drivers see in their rearview mirrors as the unit approaches.

with its front bumper downrigger, the KME units had an under-bumper scissors jack.

In 1996, KME began to redesign the mid-mount aerial platform to address the need for a five-section, 95-foot unit to better compete with other products in the industry. A fifth section would reduce the overall length of the vehicle, so KME added an additional fly while modifying the other sections, and in 1997 brought to market a unit with a 1,000-pound dry rating and a 500-pound wet rating, similar to the other mid-mount aerial platform that the company offered. KME redesigned the torque box in such a way as to eliminate the need for the front bumper–mounted scissors jack. The new unit had the same 18-foot spread as the other platform with only the four outriggers.

In 1996, KME received a substantial order for fire apparatus from the Los Angeles County Fire Department. In response to this order, KME modified the three-section, 75-foot aerial and mounted it on a trailer to implement its first TDA. KME also mounted a pump and water tank on the tractor to produce a tiller quint. This shared the 500-pound wet and dry ratings of the single-axle, 75-foot rear-mount with the same two outriggers and 14-foot jack spread. Nine of these were built for Los Angeles County and delivered in 1998. KME followed the 75-foot TDA with a four-section, 100-foot model. A heavier base section was added under the three-section, 75-foot aerial, which gave it a 500-pound dry rating and a 250-pound wet rating. The first 100-foot TDA went to South County, California, in 1998 and four were delivered to Los Angeles County in 1999. The 100-foot utilized two H-style outriggers with a 16-foot jack spread. Both the 75-foot and the 100-foot units could carry up to 300 gallons of water and were offered with pumps having capacities of up to 2,250 gallons per minute.

In 1997, KME used the four-section, 100-foot ladder that was developed for the TDA and developed a short wheelbase, 100-foot, rear-mounted aerial ladder with a 500-pound wet and dry rating. The ladder was mounted to the same tandem-axle chassis that KME used for the 75-foot ladder with a 750-pound rating. The new 100-foot used the two rear outriggers and two front downriggers, like the 75-foot unit. The only difference was an increased jack spread from 14 feet to 18 feet. The first aerial of this design went to Perth Amboy, New Jersey, in 2000. This was now the third 100-foot, rear-mount ladder that KME had in the line. The models available had 500-, 750-, or 1,000-pound dry ratings built with four, four, and three sections, respectively.

Also in 1997, KME found the need for another mid-mount aerial platform smaller than those that were already in its product mix. By shortening each of the five ladder sections, KME developed an 81-foot platform with the same tip loads, torque box, outriggers, and jack spread as the other two KME mid-mount aerial platforms. The first 81-foot platform was sold to Harrisburg, Pennsylvania, for delivery in 2002.

In 1999, KME introduced a second mid-mount aerial ladder to the line-up. The 500-pound, four-section, 100-foot ladder was released in a mid-mount design. This offered a 500-pound tip load, wet and dry, with a travel height of 9 feet, 4 inches. It shared the four outriggers and 18-foot jack spread of the rear-mount. The first ladder of this style was sold to the Thompsonville Fire Department, Ladder Company 1 of Enfield, Connecticut, in 2000. This was the same fire company that purchased the first Grumman 92-foot, mid-mount aerial platform in 1987.

In 1999, KME released a five-section, 100-foot, mid-mount aerial platform. This unit had a 1,000-pound dry rating and a 500-pound wet rating. It utilized four H-style outriggers with an 18-foot spread. The first 100-foot mid-mount platform was delivered in 1999 to Plainfield, New Jersey.

Ladder Towers, Inc. (LTI) – (Simon-Ladder Towers)

In 1990, the 75-foot aerial was beefed up from a 400-pound tip load to a 500-pound capacity. This became part of the AH (Aerial Heavy) Series and was offered in rear-mount and mid-mount configurations. The midship model was offered with a four-section ladder while the rear-mount utilized a three-section design. The rear-mount utilized one set of out and down stabilizers with a 16-foot spread.

In 1991, the QS Series changed from 106- and 110-foot lengths to 100 and 104 feet with and without waterways, respectively. The 106- and 110-foot designs were discontinued. The reason for this change was twofold. First was the desire for a more efficient overall tiller length, and second was a marketing decision to put forward a 100-foot aerial, which was the industry standard. The new lengths were achieved by adjusting the lengths of the existing ladder sections.

In 1991, the Atlanta Fire Department wanted a mid-mount aerial that was shorter overall than the QS-100. LTI built the first 250-pound tip load QS-90 mid-mount to satisfy this request with a serial number of 9102690. Later, the QS-90 was added to the line as a TDA. The tractor-drawn selections were vast. They included the 90-foot, 100-foot, and 104-foot QS styles with 250-pound tip loads. These utilized two H-style outriggers with a 16-foot spread. There were also 100-foot and 110-foot QH models that had a 500-pound tip load with two swing-out style outriggers and an 18-foot spread.

In 1994, LTI released the LT-102, which replaced the ST2000. The LT-102 was a new ladder with redesigned

sections. The sides of the base section had plates from the rear end to a point just beyond the lifting cylinder attachment structure. The midsection side rails had plates from the rear to an area roughly one-third from the top of this section. This design characteristic corrected the deflection of the ladder and added rigidity without adding much extra weight. In addition, the spot at which the lift cylinders met the base section was raised to a point at the top of the

LTI offered three styles of ladder towers during the 1990s. The 75-foot LT-75, the 85-foot HT-85, and the 102-foot LT-102 shown here for Central Stickney, Illinois; Indianapolis, Indiana; and Cleveland, Ohio, were all displayed at the FDIC in Indianapolis. The LT-75 was later renamed the HT-75 because it shared noticeable characteristics with the HT-85 and not the LT-102. The LT-102 utilizes the TLC configuration at the top of the base section where the other two units have lifting points below the base section. Each of the units in the photo features a different configuration of the Simon-Duplex D9400 cab.

This 75-foot quint was built for the High Point, North Carolina, fire department in 1995. The unit has a 1,500 gallon-per-minute pump and carries 400 gallons of water on an HME 1871 Series chassis. Dual sirens and air horns are recessed into the bumper. Older units had the siren in the cab face or on the roof with the air horns. Lowering these items to the bumper reduced the noise and provided a safer environment for the firefighters in the cab.

The first full tiller quint that LTI built was delivered to the Huntington Beach Fire Department in California. A 1,500 gallon-per-minute pump and 187-gallon water tank were added to the rear of the Simon-Duplex D8400 tractor. The QS-90 ladder has a 250-pound tip load rating, and the pre-connected attack lines are located on the trailer to keep the length of the tractor down. This configuration allowed for the great maneuverability and versatility of a tiller with the capabilities of a conventional straight frame quint apparatus.

handrails. This gave an 80-degree elevation instead of the previous 75-degree elevation and resulted in an additional 2 feet of height. Water flow capacity from the platform was 2,000 gallons per minute. The outriggers and torque box remained the same, and the platform load was still 1,000 pounds.

Shortly after the LT-102 was released, LTI introduced the AH-100 and the AH-110 rear-mount aerials. Unlike the AH-75, these longer ladders were a new design. Both were offered with pre-piped waterways. The AH-100 had a 750-pound dry rating and a 600-pound wet rating. Both ladders had four sections, although those of the 110-foot ladder were longer. The 100-foot model allowed for a shorter overall vehicle. When built without a pump, the ladder would not extend past the bumper in the travel position. When

built with a pump and extended cab, the ladder would not extend past the windshield. Jack spread was 16 feet utilizing four H-style outriggers. Shortly after the rear-mounts were introduced, LTI offered an AH-100 tractor-drawn ladder. A 750-pound AH-Series ladder was easily distinguished at a glance from other ladders due to the triangulated lifting configuration (TLC). The TLC incorporated a triangular shaped steel frame along the side of the base section surrounding the lift cylinders. These units required two sets of H-style outriggers.

Also in 1994, LTI built their first tiller quint for Huntington Beach, California. This was a QS-90 aerial with a 1,500 gallon-per-minute pump and 150-gallon water tank added to the tractor. As the quint concept gained in popularity, fire departments began looking for something that would include a pump and tank, plus the maneuverability of a TDA. Another tiller quint was built shortly thereafter for Encinitas, California.

In 1995, LTI introduced the LT-75. This was a three-section, 75-foot, rear-mounted ladder tower with a 40-foot overall length. It was rated at 1,000 pounds wet or dry with a 16-foot jack spread. Water flow capacity from the bucket was 1,500 gallons per minute. Seven of these units have been built to date, several of which had rear steering axles. This was the only 75-foot, rear-mounted platform aerial on the market. The first unit went to the Central Stickney Fire Department in Illinois with serial number 9400476.

The third rear-mount ladder tower that was available was the HT-85. This was a three-section tower with an 800-pound platform load, 85 feet of vertical reach, and the capacity to flow 1,500 gallons per minute from the platform. Similar to the LT-75, the HT-85 had a 16-foot spread with four outriggers.

The LT-75 model designation was changed to HT-75 in 1996 because it was a smaller version of the HT-85 and did not have features like the other LT models.

In 1996, LTI came out with the MMLT-93, a five-section, 93-foot, mid-mount ladder tower. It was rated at 1,000 pounds dry and 500 pounds wet. The jack spread was 16 feet for the two rear outriggers, 18 feet for the two midship outriggers; the unit also required scissors jacks under the front bumper for stabilization. The first unit went to Northport, New York, with a serial number of 9503320. LTI also offered the MMLT-75, a 75-foot, mid-mount platform aerial. This unit had a 1,000-pound rating wet or dry, with downriggers in place of the rear outriggers. The first MMLT-75 went to the Third District Volunteer Fire Department in Bristol Township, Pennsylvania, with serial number 9506619.

Also in 1996, LTI beefed up the AH-75 again to a 600-pound dry tip load with improvements to the torque box and the addition of two midship downriggers. This was available with a single or tandem rear axle chassis. The 500-pound wet rating remained the same. Pump and aerial operations could be handled by one firefighter at the pump panel. The 600-pound rating could also be achieved with a tandem-axle chassis without the midship downriggers.

The TDA selection included QS-Series 250-pound medium-duty ladders, the QH-Series 500-pound heavy-duty ladders, plus the AH-Series TLC 750-pound extra heavy-duty ladder. Stabilizers varied, with spreads of as little as 14 feet from two H-style outriggers with four lockout cylinders to secure the fifth wheel of the tractor. These cylinders tied the tractor and trailer together as a more stable base for the aerial operations with the QS ladders, compared to the standard two outriggers with a 16-foot spread. AH ladders used four outriggers with a 16-foot spread, or the optional swing-out style outriggers, which were less popular.

In 1998, Simon sold LTI to Aerial Innovations, which was jointly owned by American LaFrance and the original AI founders. LTI was then joined with the other acquired companies to achieve the status of full-line apparatus manufacturer. The corporate name was changed from Simon-Ladder Towers to Ladder Towers, Inc., doing business as American LaFrance Aerials.

Pierce

Pierce's long-range plan was to manufacture its own ladders, giving them control over the aerial engineering. In 1991, Pierce left Smeal to produce ladders on its own. This occurred at the same time that the new NFPA requirements called for minimum 250-pound tip loads. It was an awkward time for a transition and resulted in Pierce having to retrofit tandem axles under some of the single-axle units because they were overweight.

Pierce designed the new aerials in 1991, production began in 1992, and they began to ship in 1993. The ladder sections were built in Kewaunee, Wisconsin, by Kewaunee Engineering, and assembled at the Pierce facility in Appleton, Wisconsin. The new aerials were called Pierce Aerial Ladders (PAL), and at the onset they were offered as 75-foot and 105-foot rear-mount aerials only. Tip loads were increased to 500 pounds, wet or dry. Stabilizers and jack spread per item matched the Smeal ladders with two jacks and a 16-foot spread for the 75-foot ladder, and four jacks with a 14-foot spread for the 105-foot ladder. The first 105-foot PAL was job number E7612, and the first 75-foot PAL was job number E7613. Both units were built in 1993. At the same time, Pierce made the 105-foot rear-mount available with a 750-pound dry tip load rating. This was the same 105-foot aerial with an increased jack spread of 16 feet to achieve the required stability. The difference between the 500- and 750-pound rating was a stability issue as opposed to a structural issue. The 55-foot model that Pierce offered from Smeal was not part of the PAL program due to minimal demand for the smaller units.

The Pierce Quantum chassis rides a little higher than others and provides a flat floor throughout the cab. Air actuated fold-down steps are at each of the cab doors and roll down automatically when the door is opened. When a door is closed, the steps fold back up into the stored position, leaving a clean façade outside. The Oshkosh, Wisconsin, fire department is shown here with its 75-foot aerial at a fire scene. Since the driver's door is open, this step is in the down position, whereas the rear step is visible in the upright position. The extended front bumper has a large inlet plus a pre-connected trash line for small fires.

The 105-foot Pierce aerial platform was heavy and expensive. Fire departments were specifying the industry standard 100-foot aerials when going out for bids, and this put Pierce at a disadvantage in terms of overall weight and price. In 1991, Pierce redesigned the aerial platform and shortened it. As it turned out, the additional 5 feet of reach was not a substantial selling point to many fire departments. In 1991, Pierce introduced a totally redesigned 100-foot aerial platform. The platform had a capacity of 1,000 pounds dry, 600 pounds wet, and was constructed with solid panel sides. Jack spread was 18 feet with four H-style outriggers.

In the early 1990s, the makers of the Bronto Skylift, an aerial device built in Finland, were looking for a U.S. distributor and approached Pierce. In 1993, Pierce delivered its first F111-HDT 1,000-pound Bronto SkyLift on a Lance chassis to Bohemia, New York. Pierce offered the HDA, HDT, and HLA Bronto product lines in the United States with lengths ranging from 91 feet to 220 feet. Pierce continued distributing Bronto Skylifts until 1996 when Federal Signal Corporation, the parent company of E-ONE, purchased Bronto. A total of six Bronto Skylifts with Pierce bodies and chassis were manufactured and sold. Two were 111-foot HDT units going to Bohemia and Wading River, both on Long Island. One 167-foot HLA was shipped to South Padre Island with three rear axles, and the other three were 134-foot units going to South Hampton, Long Island; Beltsville, Maryland; and the Cincinnati-Northern Kentucky Airport.

In 1993, Pierce came out with a super heavy-duty, 100-foot ladder. It had a 1,500-pound dry tip load, a 1,250-pound wet rating, and an 18-foot spread. This was an aerial platform without the bucket. The first super heavy-duty ladder went to the Brentwood Fire District in Brentwood, New York, with job number E8001. Pierce was still offering the complete line of Snorkel products including the 50-, 65-, and 75-foot Tele-Squrts, the 54-foot Squrt, plus 55-, 65-, 75-, and 85-foot Snorkels.

In 1996, when this unit was built, Pierce was the U.S. distributor for the Bronto Skylift aerials from Finland. Although only six combination Pierce-Bronto units were manufactured, three of them were delivered on Long Island, including this unit in Wading River. Delivered in 1994 on a Lance chassis, this is a 111-foot, three-boom HDT Series unit. Due to the design of the boom and the side stacking of the ground ladders, compartment space in the body was limited.

In 1994, Pierce introduced 75-foot and 100-foot medium-duty aerials. These lighter weight ladders had dry tip loads of 250 pounds and were more economical than the heavier aerials. Both required only one set of H-style outriggers, with a 12-foot spread for the 75-foot aerial, and a 16-foot spread on most 100-foot aerials. The aerials were designed to flow 1,000 gallons of water per minute, while fully extended at zero degrees of elevation without a firefighter at the tip.

Pierce replaced the 105-foot TDA, which had been out of the line since the company left Smeal, with a new medium-duty, 100-foot model in 1994. This was a four-section aerial with a 250-pound tip load at zero degrees and a 500-pound rating above 39 degrees. Pierce no longer used the swing-out stabilizers, opting instead for one set of H-style outriggers located at the turntable with a 16-foot spread.

Oshkosh Truck purchased Pierce in 1996. In 1997, Pierce introduced the Dash 2000 chassis, offering a greater cramp angle and a larger cab with more visibility. Also in 1997, Pierce introduced a new bucket for the aerial platforms. The bucket offered 22 square feet of space, making it the largest and widest in the industry. The new platform also was equipped for life saving accessories, including a stokes basket mount, winch, a life ladder for extending over a parapet wall, and rappelling arms for rescue work.

In 1998, Oshkosh acquired Nova Quintech, a Canadian manufacturer of aerial devices. Pierce acquired the designs, engineering, technology, patents, and on-hand inventory. The first several units that Pierce completed were part of

Firefighters from the Tallman Volunteer Fire Department in New York demonstrate the stability of their new Pierce aerial platform and the large amount of space in the bucket for four firefighters with full gear and tools. The solid panels on either side of the twin nozzles have hinged doors, providing a means of egress to the roof. This particular aerial has a 2000 gallon-per-minute pump and no water tank. From this angle, it is easy to note that the extra-long Lance cab is a split tilt-cab. Also visible from this vantage is 1,000 feet of large-diameter, 5-inch supply hose, which can be dropped to get water from a hydrant and allows the truck to operate without tying up a pumper.

the Nova Quintech backlog for other OEMs. Two units with bodywork by 3D and a third that was sold through RD Murray were in progress when the sale of the company was consummated. At the time of the purchase, Nova Quintech had OEM alliances with 3D, Alexis, Darley, and RD Murray. Nova's product line included the Sky-Five, the Sky-Four, the Sky-Pod,

the Sky-Boom, and the Sky-Arm—which was one of the principal products of interest to Pierce. The Sky-Arm was a 100-foot, four-section, telescoping aerial platform with an articulating fly section. The tip load was 500 pounds wet and 750 pounds dry. The Sky-Five was a five-section, 100-foot aerial ladder that was offered as a rear-mount or midship model. It had a 750-pound dry tip load and a 500-pound wet rating. The Sky-Four was a four-section, 100-foot aerial ladder similar to the Sky-Five. The Sky-Pod was a three-section, 103-foot aerial platform with a dry rating of 1,000 pounds. The Sky-Boom was a two-section, telescoping waterway with an aluminum rescue ladder similar to the Tele-Squrt, and was the other product that Pierce was eager to acquire since the Snorkel line had been incorporated into the American LaFrance family that same year. Two Sky-Boom models were available; one had a 55-foot length and the other reached 61 feet. Both were rated at 500 pounds dry and 250 pounds wet, and used two rear-mounted, A-style stabilizers with a spread of 11 feet, 11 inches.

Pierce had no mid-mount aerial ladder during this time frame and acquired a Sky-Five mid-mount with no body on a Spartan chassis through the purchase of Nova Quintech. The ladder was remounted onto a Pierce chassis and was offered as part of the aerial family. The unit was not popular, no orders were received, and the demo was never sold.

Two Pierce 100-foot platform aerials work at an extra alarm fire. The truck in the foreground is a 1993 unit on a Pierce Arrow chassis. Since the outriggers lifted the rig off the ground, the operator used a slide-out shelf so that he could have a comfortable position to access the controls at the pump panel. A fold-down step at the rear made it easier to climb up to the turntable. Metal wheel chocks were positioned around the front tires as an added safety measure against movement of the unit, and steel locking pins were inserted into the vertical shaft of the outriggers in the unlikely event of multiple system failures. The tower on the other side of the fire is a 1991 model.

The unit became a loaner and rental unit for Pierce customers who found themselves without a Pierce ladder in the event of an accident or other such circumstances .

Pierce added an 85-foot aerial platform in 1998 that debuted at the Fire Department Instructor's Conference (FDIC) in Indianapolis. This three-section aerial used four H-style outriggers with a 16-foot spread, and had a 1,000-pound dry rating with a 500-pound wet rating. The first unit built for a customer went to Springfield, Oregon.

In 1999, Oshkosh purchased Kewaunee Engineering, the company that fabricated Pierce aerial ladder sections, and it became Kewaunee Fabrications.

R.K. Aerials

In 1988, Maxim fabricated its own 250-pound aerial ladders, but it wanted something stronger without having to invest in a total redesign. Maxim enlisted the services of a welder from Smeal Fire Apparatus and asked him to build a heavy-duty 500-pound tip load aerial for Maxim. At that time, he left to begin his own company, R.K. Aerials, with the promise of 18 aerials per year to be purchased by Maxim. In 1989, two were built and mounted on Pemfab

Few large modern aerial ladders are ordered on commercial chassis, such as this tandem-axle Freightliner FL80, although it can provide a substantial price savings for the fire department. This 1999 aerial for the City of Nevada Fire Department in Missouri features a 75-foot ladder by R.K. Aerials. Central States built the body, featuring rollup doors, a 500-gallon water tank, and a 1,500 gallon-per-minute pump. The bumper was fitted to accommodate the air horns and the mechanical siren.

chassis with Maxim bodywork before Maxim went bankrupt and closed at the end of that year. These were four-section, steel, 109-foot, rear-mounted ladders with a tip load of 500 pounds while flowing 1,000 gallons of water per minute. One of these two aerials went to the fire department in Middletown, Rhode Island. A third ladder had been built for Maxim but was never mounted on a truck. In late 1989 or early 1990, after the Pierre Thibault Company had closed its doors, R.K. Aerials was approached by Thibault to mount the 109-foot ladder on a chassis that Thibault already had, which included outriggers and a torque box. The sale of this unit kept R.K. Aerials in business.

During 1991 and 1992, Ferrara Fire Apparatus approached R.K. Aerials and requested a 75-foot ladder. This unit marked the beginning of a long relationship between the two companies. The first unit, which went to the Apolusia, Louisiana, fire department, was a quint built on a Spartan chassis. The three-section ladder had a 500-pound tip load while flowing 1,000 gallons per minute and used two rear H-style outriggers. Roughly six months later, R.K. Aerials was approached by Central States Fire Apparatus to build a 60-foot aerial device for one of its customers. R.K. Aerial's production went from six aerials in 1993 to 37 aerials in 2000.

In the mid-1990s, other body builders came to R.K. wanting to add aerials to their own product offerings. These included W.S. Darley, Spencer Manufacturing, and Toyne. In 1997, R.K. Aerials sold its first units for delivery overseas.

The R.K. Aerials product line included rear-mounted, straight stick aerial ladders in lengths of 50, 60, 65, 75, 85, and 109 feet. The two-section 50-foot, 60-foot, and 65-foot models rode on a single-axle chassis. The three-section 65-foot, 75-foot, and 85-foot models could use a single- or tandem-axle chassis, while the four-section, 109-foot required a tandem axle. There was also a four-section, 75-foot, rearmount, straight aerial ladder. The two-section models had one set of H-style outriggers at the rear with a 14-foot spread. The 75-foot rearmount utilized one set of rear H-style outriggers with a 16-foot spread. The 85-foot and the 109-foot rear-mounts had two sets of H-style outriggers with a 16-foot spread for stability. All of the ladders were available with a pre-piped waterway. The pre-piped waterway could be pinned at the fly section or midsection to facilitate rescue operations. All of these aerials offered a 500-pound tip

Ferrara sold ladders from R.K. Aerials for several years. The company also worked closely with Spartan and then HME to provide a proprietary cab and chassis for Ferrara customers. This 1999 unit from Leavenworth, Kansas, has a 75-foot R.K. ladder, a 1,250 gallon-per-minute pump, 300 gallons of water, and an HME 1871P cab and chassis. It is first due at the U.S. Penitentiary at Leavenworth.

load while flowing water. R.K. Aerials were built with a detachable egress ladder at the tip of the fly section to minimize down time and repair costs in the event of accidental damage to this section. Ladder controls were at the turntable for 75-foot and longer ladders, with an option to duplicate the controls at the pump panel.

Mid-mount straight aerial ladders were offered in two-section, 50-foot; three-section 65-foot; and four-section 75-foot models. The outriggers, waterway, chassis considerations, and tip loads were the same as for the rear-mounted units. All R.K. Aerials could be outfitted with blue marker lights along the inside rails of the base section to illuminate the ladder rungs.

The product line also included four aerial platforms. There was an 85-foot and a 104-foot rear-mount unit, as well as an 85-foot and 95-foot mid-mount. All were rated at 1,000 pounds dry and 500 pounds while flowing 1,500 gallons of water per minute. The aerial platforms had two sets of H-style outriggers with an 18-foot spread. The 85-foot rear-mount model had three sections and the other three units had four-section designs. All used a platform with 18

square feet of space with a single deck gun as standard, plus an option for a second one.

All of the straight ladders and aerial platform devices could be ordered in the industry standard color of white, or special ordered in silver. The R.K. Aerials were available on both commercial chassis as well as custom fire truck chassis from HME, Spartan, and in the case of Ferrara, the Inferno chassis. All R.K. Aerials were built with a torque box frame that was bolted directly to the chassis frame rails.

At the 1999 FRI convention in Kansas City, Ferrara informed R.K. Aerials that it would be buying aerials from a different supplier from that point forward. Ferrara/R.K. units would be delivered for the next year or so until the backlog of orders was fulfilled.

Schwing

The Schwing divisions around the world were best known for their work with the concrete placement industry. Schwing built articulated booms for placing concrete at construction sites in areas too difficult for a concrete mixer to reach and too cumbersome for placement by workers with wheelbarrows. Schwing was founded in 1934 and began producing truck-mounted booms in 1968. Building on the articulated boom design used in the U.S. fire service since the late 1950s, Schwing Siwa, Sao Paulo, Brazil, produced the first GMB Series articulating aerial platform for fire fighting in 1983. This was a three-section, 95-foot boom with a platform rated at 770 pounds and capable of discharging 1,000 gallons of water per minute. Then, in 1985, the German division of Schwing introduced the first GMB 28 articulating platform. The GMB 34 was added in 1988, also in Germany. This model featured a 115-foot, multiple arm boom with a platform.

Schwing also produced a line of articulating, elevated master stream devices. These units made up the GLA Series. In 1991, Schwing America built its first 56-foot GLA unit. This line was expanded in 1993 with the introduction of the GLA 85 high-flow boom. This unit had an 85-foot reach accomplished with a three-section articulating boom.

The GLA 85 high-flow boom had a 5,000 gallon-per-minute discharge capacity, the first of its kind in the fire service. The pre-piped waterway utilized 6-inch-diameter piping. A chemical company in Corpus Christi, Texas, purchased the first unit of this model in 1995.

The GMB and GLA Series devices were available on any custom fire truck or heavy-duty commercial chassis specified by the purchaser, and could be accommodated by most fire apparatus body builders. Each unit required a tandem-axle chassis and utilized four H-style outriggers with a spread of 19 feet, 8 inches; 24 feet, 4 inches; or 27 feet, 11 inches, depending on the model.

In 1995, Schwing sold its first GMB 34 Series, four-section, 115-foot articulating platform aerial. This three-section aerial was mounted on an HME 1871 LMFDSC Series chassis with bodywork by 3D, and was purchased by the Carlstadt Fire Department in New Jersey. While the vertical reach was 115 feet, the horizontal reach was only 73 feet. The platform had a rated capacity of 800 pounds with a 1,300 gallon-per-minute capacity. Four H-style outriggers stabilized the truck with a 20-foot spread in the rear and 17-foot spread in the front. This was a midship-mounted aerial device, where the platform tucked in underneath the boom and hung at the rear of the truck, unlike other articulated boom platform aerials that extended over the cab when nested.

The GLA product line as of 1996 was expanded to include 53, 92, 106, 140, and 170 feet in height with 1,600 gallon-per-minute capacities. The number of boom sections was 2, 3, 4, 4, and 4, respectively. These units could also be mounted onto fireboats.

In 1997, Schwing incorporated radio remote control availability for the boom and monitor. At the same time, the waterway piping was enlarged from 6 to 8 inches.

Seagrave

Seagrave was an OEM partner with Snorkel dating back to the 1960s. In addition to the Seagrave aerials, dealers were authorized to represent the Snorkel product line featuring the Squrt, Tele-Squrt, and Snorkel. Many of these units were produced on Seagrave custom chassis during this period. Although the popularity of ladder towers seriously affected sales of Snorkel articulating platforms, many loyal customers continued to order these aerials from the OEM builder of their choice; the Baltimore City Fire Department, for example, purchased an 85-foot Seagrave Snorkel in 1994.

In 1992, new specifications for aerial ladder weight ratings from the NFPA went into effect. Prior to this time, specific tip load capacities were not required, only performance criteria. The new NFPA guidelines specified a minimum tip load rating of 250 pounds.

The Rear Admiral Series that Seagrave had been manufacturing for 30 years did not specify tip load ratings. In response to the NFPA guidelines, Seagrave retired the Rear Admiral Series and introduced the Patriot Series aerials. These new ladders featured double web, hollow I-beam construction base rails and provided Seagrave with a 250-pound and greater tip load ladder. The Patriot Series featured hydraulic extension cylinders for the ladder, replacing the winch-type extension on the Rear Admiral Series.

The 250-pound rear-mount now used two H-style outriggers at the rear of the unit, instead of the A-style jacks that were common for the Rear Admiral. The 100-foot, rear-mount aerial and the 100-foot, tractor-drawn ladders were now part of the Patriot Series. The first Patriot went to Cicero, Illinois.

The four-section, 100-foot TDAs had the option of a pre-piped waterway. Aerials built with a waterway required the installation of two midship, H-style outriggers replacing the A-style outriggers that were still standard for the tiller.

In the early 1990s, Seagrave wanted to enter the aerial platform market. The company hired an engineer named Ken Merica, formerly of SFI, the designer of the original Pierce aerial platform. The product he designed for Seagrave emerged in 1992 as the Apollo, a three-section, 105-foot aerial platform. The Apollo utilized four H-style outriggers with a spread of 17 feet, 10 inches, and was offered exclusively on a Seagrave custom chassis. Both the conventional J-Series cab and the low-profile L-Series cabs were available. Single or dual turrets were offered at the bucket with a maximum output of 2,000 gallons per minute. The first Apollo aerial platform went to the Glenn Dale Fire Department in Prince George's County, Maryland, with no pump or water tank. Tip load for the Apollo was 1,000 pounds dry and 550 pounds while flowing water.

Seagrave offered a 75-foot Patriot rear-mounted aerial on a single-axle pumper chassis in 1996. The P-75 had a 500-pound tip load rating and used two rear, H-style outriggers. The ladder controls were placed at the pump panel with an option for placement at the rear step. There were no controls at the turntable, nor was there a conventional, truck-type turntable base. The P-75 could be ordered with either a Hale or Waterous pump and up to a 500-gallon water tank. This unit was basically a first out engine company with a 75-foot rescue ladder and remote controlled waterway to compete with products offered by other companies; it carried an engine's complement of ground ladders. The

The area around Louisville, Kentucky, has a heavy concentration of Seagrave apparatus. With several units already in their firehouse, the Fern Creek Fire Department took delivery in 1999 of this 100-foot Patriot aerial with a 500-pound tip load. Two rear H-style outriggers stabilize the four-section ladder with two additional midship-mounted A-style jacks that do not extend past the body of the vehicle when extended. A Patriot ordered without the midship A-style jacks has a smaller, 250-pound tip load.

One of the first 105-foot Apollo platform aerials by Seagrave was built in 1993 for the fire department in Fitchburg, Wisconsin. This unit had no pump or water tank and featured a low-profile cab with raised roof areas over each of the rear crew doors. This truck was outfitted for a single-master stream in the platform.

first P-75 was delivered to the Fairmont Hahntown Volunteer Fire Department in North Huntingdon, Pennsylvania.

In 1997, Seagrave unveiled the Mean Stick. This was a 75-foot quint with a 500-pound tip load, a short 192-inch wheelbase, 136 cubic feet of storage space, a 500-gallon water tank, and 115 feet of enclosed ground-ladder storage. Contrasting the P-75, the Mean Stick carried a truck complement of ground ladders in a short quint. Like a truck, the ladder controls were placed at the full size turntable. There was an option for a duplicate set of controls at the pump panel or at the tip of the fly section. The Riverhead, New York, fire department received the first Mean Stick. Seagrave also offered a low-profile chassis option with a 75-foot ladder. This configuration altered the available compartment space from what the Mean Stick package provided and was called instead a 75-foot Patriot ladder.

Also at that time, the Patriot Series 100-foot, rearmount aerial line was increased to include a 500-pound-capacity unit in addition to the 250-pound model. The jack spread for this unit was 16 feet and it utilized two H-style jacks and two modified A-frame jacks.

In 1998, Seagrave discontinued the RA110 aerial. In 1999, the parent company of FWD Seagrave purchased the Aerialscope product line from Baker, which had declared bankruptcy. As a sister company to FWD Seagrave, Aerialscope was a separate company handling its own sales,

marketing, and production. Chassis for the Aerialscope tower ladder were available from Seagrave or Spartan.

Smeal

In 1992, after the company no longer supplied aerial ladders to Pierce, Smeal concentrated on selling a complete line of fire apparatus under its own name. Smeal developed an 85-foot aerial platform and followed that in 1993 with a 100-foot platform. Both units had 1,000-pound dry tip loads and 500-pound wet ratings with single or dual monitors. The bucket offered 21 square feet of space for firefighters with gear. Stability was achieved with four H-style outriggers with a 16-foot spread for the 85-foot unit and an 18-foot spread for the 100-foot unit. Unlike those of other companies, the front outriggers on the Smeal aerial platforms were mounted just behind the cab and forward of the pump to enhance leveling capabilities.

The aerial ladder line consisted of 55-foot, 75-foot, and 105-foot rear-mounted models. Each unit was rated at 500 pounds dry or while flowing 1,250 gallons per minute at the tip. The 55-foot model used two H-style rear jacks with a 14-foot spread. The 75-foot unit used two rear H-style jacks as standard, but had an option for two downriggers mounted directly behind the cab for added stability. The 105-foot unit required four H-style outriggers and had an 18-foot spread.

The attractiveness of the Snorkel articulating platform aerial has been greatly affected in the past 10 years by the popularity of tower ladders. Still, they fill a niche for a handful of fire departments each year. One such customer was the Broomall Fire Company of Pennsylvania, which ordered this 85-foot Snorkel in 1999 on an HME 1871 chassis with bodywork by M&W, a small apparatus builder. The body was designed with a hydraulic ladder rack, allowing for out-of-the-way ground-ladder storage that does not inhibit the amount of compartment space. Wheel chocks are conveniently stored on each side of the front tires.

Smeal aerial characteristics included a torque box bolted directly to the chassis frame, providing for a rigid unit. The torque box also enabled the unit to carry ground ladders down the center of the body with access from the rear. Smeal also offered a computerized system to monitor the load on the ladder during operations. The system had provisions to factor in the distributed load including equipment, ice, and other conditions that could affect the weight on the ladder. Smeal pioneered its "Ergonomic Hose Load" option for rear-mounted 55-foot and 75-foot aerials. This was a large, hydraulically operated, slide-out tray to simplify the reloading of large-diameter hose after a fire. Up to 1,000 feet of 5-inch hose could be carried in the hose bed, which was tucked inside the torque box when stored. Another popular option for hose storage was the "E-Z Load" design, which permitted access to the hose bed while the aerial ladder was bedded. Smeal also offered a non-glare system of blue lights to assist firefighters with orientation on the ladder during operations where visibility might be obstructed by smoke or other impairments.

In 1994, Smeal designed a rear-mounted, 100-foot aerial ladder to fit into a firehouse with a 10-foot door. This was a four-section unit with a 500-pound dry rating and a 250-pound wet rating. It used four H-style outriggers with a 16-foot spread. The UT100 was a redesigned ladder that included a readjustment in the angle of the lift cylinders. The first UT100 was built on a Simon-Duplex chassis for the department in Middlesborough, Kentucky.

In 1998, Smeal introduced a super heavy-duty, 100-foot, rear-mounted aerial ladder, with a 1,500-pound tip load wet or dry. This was a three-section aerial with four H-style outriggers and a spread of 18 feet. Lawrence, Kansas, received the first Smeal super heavy-duty ladder on an HME chassis.

Smeal also introduced a 100-foot mid-mount ladder in 1998. This was a five-section aerial with four stabilizers. Two midship, H-style jacks with an 18-foot spread plus two rear downriggers supported the aerial operations. The tip load was 500 pounds dry or while flowing up to 1,000 gallons of water per minute. The mid-mount ladder could accommodate pumps that were rated up to 2,000 gallons per minute and water tanks with as much as 500-gallon capacities. The first five-section mid-mount went to Canton, Massachusetts.

In 1999, Smeal added an 85-foot, mid-mount platform aerial. This unit offered a 1,000-pound tip load while dry and a 500-pound rating while flowing 1,500 gallons of water per minute. It featured a Waterous pump and a water tank capable of holding up to 400 gallons of water. The mid-mount used four H-style outriggers with an 18-foot spread. The steel ladder consisted of four sections and the platform offered 17 square feet of space and one monitor nozzle. The first delivery of a mid-mount platform went to the East Moriches Fire Department in Long Island, New York.

Snorkel

Snorkel upgraded the Tele-Squrt 50 in 1994 to increase the inside ladder width, increase the jack spread to 11 feet, 4 inches, and increase the degree of lateral movement for the nozzle. Also, the water pipe on each side of the boom was increased in size, and the unit controls were changed from three levers to a single lever.

In 1996, Snorkel upgraded several aspects of the three-section TS-65 (Tele-Squrt 65). Among the changes were a wider stabilizer spread of 11 feet, 9 inches, an increase in the space between ladder rails, and a change in the rated load above 45 degrees from 800 pounds to 750 pounds to comply with NFPA 1901. Snorkel also had to raise the handrails to 12 inches on all of the Tele-Squrt ladders as a result of the regulation. Each of the Tele-Squrt models was now offered

Saulsbury built this 65-foot Tele-Squrt on a Simon-Duplex D9400 chassis in 1996 for the fire department in Highland, Indiana. It is equipped with a 2,000 gallon-per-minute pump and carries 750 gallons of water in addition to 30 gallons each of type A and B foam. The pump is located at the rear of the unit with Saulsbury's electronic, diagrammatic pump panel, which includes a color-coded diagram depicting the layout of each intake and discharge for ease of operation. The placement of the operator's panel opposite the driver's side is a safety measure to keep the pump operator on the curb side of the vehicle and out of traffic.

with optional fold-down handrails to lower the travel height of the unit by 7 inches.

Snorkel ownership changed in 1997 when the company was sold to Omniquip. In August of 1998, the fire service products became part of American LaFrance, now a division of the Freightliner Corporation. As of this writing, the Snorkel Company built industrial man lifts under the name Snorkel-lift, and was no longer involved in the fire service market.

In 1998, the TS-75 (Tele-Squrt 75) underwent considerable redesign and upgrades. The two sets of A-style jacks had a smaller spread of 12 feet, 3 inches. This was considerably narrower than the 15 feet, 3 inches that was required previously. The unit now had a higher tip load capacity. The new dry capacity ranged from a 500-pound tip load up to 1,000 pounds distributed load below 45 degrees of elevation in addition to a 750-pound tip load or 1,500 pounds distributed load above 45 degrees. The nested length of the unit was reduced by 3 feet, and the width of the ladder sections was increased.

Sutphen

In 1990, Sutphen added another ladder. This was a four-section, 75-foot unit that maintained all of the characteristics and features of the three-section units while offering a shorter rear overhang and a 750-pound tip load. The first four-section unit was sold to South Pasadena, Florida, in 1990.

After the last twin platform unit was produced in 1991, a new mini-tower model that utilized the single platform from the large towers was introduced and designated the MT70 or 70+. The first MT70 was shipped to Albany, New York, in 1992.

A new aerial was introduced in 1991. The model TS104 was a 104-foot, midship-mounted aerial ladder. This was a 500-pound wet or dry, four-section aluminum ladder, unlike the previous designs. The TS104 used a tandem-axle chassis with the traditional Sutphen tower stabilizers consisting of two downriggers behind the rear axles, and two H-style outriggers beneath the turntable, with an 18-foot spread. The ladder was three-sided, eliminating the top side of the standard Sutphen box design, providing an open walkway with high handrails similar in appearance to ladders built by other companies. Unlike other companies that tapered the end of the fly section, each section of the TS104 was U-shaped and squared off for the full length of the ladder. The city of Columbus, Ohio, received the first TS104. In 1992, a tractor-drawn version of the TS104 was produced. The first unit went to Nashville, Tennessee. Only three of these TDAs were produced prior to publication of this book.

In 1992, Sutphen offered the 95-foot tower ladder with a less expensive cab option to comply with regulations requiring cabs to be fully enclosed. The short four door (SFD) version simply added rear facing doors to the back of

This is a TS104 midship ladder from Sutphen with 350 gallons of water and a 1,500 gallon-per-minute pump. Built in 1995 for Highland Park, Illinois, the 104-foot aerial ladder sections are three sided, unlike the other aerial devices that Sutphen builds. Before this model was introduced in 1991, all Sutphen ladders had four-sided box boom construction with high handrails along the top of the sections. The TS104 design allowed Sutphen to lower the travel height considerably without sacrificing storage space. Sutphen's custom tilt-cab is easy to spot with the rear doors that angle back away from the turntable instead of forming the customary straight vertical line.

The Homeville Volunteer Fire Company of West Mifflin, Pennsylvania, purchased this 1998 aerial from Sutphen. It features a four-section, 75-foot aerial ladder with the standard Sutphen box boom design with high handrails. The driver's side features full, high side compartments and a five-step ladder just behind the cab to gain access to the turntable. The waterway is protected inside the boom and the extended fly section protects the remote controlled nozzle. The standard configuration for this aerial is a 1,500 gallon-per-minute pump and a 500-gallon water tank.

This is a 1999 Sutphen pumper with an MT70 mid-mounted platform aerial for Scarsdale, New York. Similar to the larger aerials, the box boom frame protects the waterway to the dual turrets at the platform. A small ladder is supplied to gain access to the turntable and the boom is equipped with an external ladder along the top. This aerial uses one set of A-style jacks under the turntable for stability.

an open canopy cab. Instead of using additional sheet metal to lengthen the cab and add the additional set of side doors, the SFD accomplished the task without added length or excessive expense to the fire department. The Orange County Fire Authority in California purchased one such unit.

The Sutphen custom tilt-cab chassis was released in 1994. The rear crew area of the cab shared the angled roof that was characteristic of Sutphen's earlier fully enclosed, medium, four-door fixed cabs. Cab options included a 10-inch raised roof. The standard cab offered a low travel height of 9 feet, 10 inches. Also in the mid-1990s, stainless steel became the standard building material for all aerial bodies.

Tory, Michigan, is home for this 1998, 100-foot, Sutphen platform aerial. Tower 38 has the high handrail option that is requested for slightly better than half of the tower orders received. The truck has a 1,500 gallon-per-minute pump and carries 300 gallons of water. The grill has been cut out to provide space for the mechanical siren.

When the 65- and 75-foot aerials were produced with an open rear jump seat prior to fully enclosed cabs, access to the turntable involved stepping up to the rear jump seat area and then continuing up a small added step that was mounted to the body. With the fully enclosed four-door cabs, Sutphen added a five-step vertical ladder immediately behind the cab to gain access to the turntable. The 75-foot midship was also offered with a fixed SFD cab featuring a raised roof area over the rear-facing jump seats. Since this cab utilized a step behind the cab for access to the seats, this was also the means of gaining access to the turntable, and the vertical ladder was omitted. This quint still used two A-style jacks with a 16-foot spread located under the turntable.

The side-door enclosed cab was modified in 1998 to include an awkward looking rear cab extension to provide additional space for seating or storage. This long medium four-door (LMFD) cab lengthened the wheelbase of the unit. The rear cab wall was straight, even though the rear door still featured the angled design.

Also in 1998, Sutphen introduced a TDA platform called the 2000+ platform tiller at the FRI trade show in Louisville. This four-section, 100-foot aluminum ladder had a unique platform design that acted as the housing for the tillerman when the ladder was bedded. The bucket floor became the ceiling for the tillerman's cab. The roof rose at the scene for deployment and transformation into the bucket. As of this writing, the unit had not generated a significant amount of interest in the industry.

In 1998, Tom Sutphen unveiled a new design in tractor-drawn aerials, a tractor-drawn platform aerial. The platform bucket doubled as the housing for the tillerman while steering the rear of the trailer. The unit sported Sutphen's trademark dual nozzles that rest on either side of the bucket at the platform. A custom tilt-cab tractor built by Sutphen pulled the unit.

CHAPTER FIVE

2000

AND INTO THE

TWENTY-FIRST CENTURY

American LaFrance

At the 2000 FDIC trade show in Indianapolis, American LaFrance introduced its newest aerial, the Metro Stick. The MS-100 was a new four-section, light-duty city aerial with a 250-pound dry rating and no weight rating at the tip while flowing water at zero degrees of elevation. It was offered on a single- or tandem-axle chassis. A single axle required four outriggers with a 12-foot spread, while a tandem axle could be outfitted with the same four or simply with two rear outriggers and a 16-foot spread. The MS and the MV shared the same outriggers as the Silver Eagle with similar torque box designs. When built with a pre-piped waterway, the Metro Stick became an MS-104. Fairview, New Jersey, received the first MS-100 with serial number 0105880 on an Eagle chassis.

During 2000, when the LTI product line was fully integrated into American LaFrance, a new system of model names and numbers was instituted. The full aerial line consisted of 30 models including the Snorkel products (four items), the Silver Eagle (one item), and the turntable ladders, a style originally designed for the export market (three items). Ladders ranged in tip load ratings from 250 pounds to 1,500 pounds dry, and 250 pounds to 1,000 pounds while flowing water.

American LaFrance Aerials; model number coding chart

First digit	Second digit	Third digit	Fourth digit	Remaining digits
Type of unit	Dry tip load	Actual number of sections	Placement of the turntable	Actual rated height of the aerial device
C=city ladder	0 = 0		R = rear-mounted	
E=Silver Eagle	1 = 250		M = mid-mounted	
K=Snorkel	2 = 500		T = tractor-drawn	
L=aerial ladder	3 = 750			
M=turntable ladder	4 = 1,000			
P=platform aerial	5 = 1,250			
S=Squrt	6 = 1,500			
T=Tele-Squrt				

Milwaukee has been adding pumpers and aerial ladders from Pierce to its fleet. Ladder 13 shown here on the scene at a pin-in accident is one of several ladders in the city that carries extrication equipment, including air bags and hydraulic tools. Milwaukee does not spec ladders with pumps or water tanks.

The table on the previous page will be helpful to decipher the model number code. The first digit represents the type of aerial, followed by the tip load dry, the number of sections, where the turntable is mounted, and finally the rated height of the device. The E23R-75 was the Silver Eagle, 500-pound, three-section, rear-mounted, 75-foot aerial ladder.

Rear-mount ladders from 55 to 75 feet were as follows: L12R-55, L23R-75, L24R-75, and L24M-75. The L23R was previously the MV ladder, while the L24 units were the QS-75 Series.

The longer rear-mount ladders were as follows: L14R-90, L14M-90, and L14R-100, all of which were the QS Series. The C14R-100 and the C14R-104 were the light-duty Metro Stick aerials with 250-pound dry tip loads and no appreciable

ratings when wet at zero degrees of elevation. The L34R-100 and L34R-110 were the AH Series and the L63R-100 was the ML Series ladder.

TDAs were the L23T-75, L34T-100, and the L34T-110 from the AH Series, while both the L14T-90 and the L14T-100 were the QS Series ladders.

Mid- and rear-mounted platforms were the P44M-75, P45M-93, and P43R-100 previously known as the LT Series, and what was formerly the HT Series became the P43R-75 and the P33R-85.

Additional aerials in the design stage for the AH Series included the L34M-100, a four-section, mid-mount aerial with a 750-pound rating and the L45M93, a five-section, mid-mount aerial with a 1,000-pound rating.

E-ONE

In March of 2000, E-ONE introduced the Side Stacker aerial body for the 75-foot aerial. This new body was designed to allow firefighters to carry 1,000 feet of 5-inch hose and be able to repack or load the hose after a fire without having to raise or move the aerial ladder out of the way. E-ONE also provided more compartment space with the Side Stacker than was available from the competition.

In March of 2001, at the FDIC trade show in Indianapolis, E-ONE introduced a new, lower cost cab and chassis called the Typhoon. The Typhoon offered seating for four to six personnel and was fully multiplexed. Unlike any of the other E-ONE custom chassis, the Typhoon was designed with a uniquely different exterior look. The other cabs offered by E-ONE maintained a smooth, contoured front design with a flat chrome grille. The Typhoon had the contoured design but the grill had a raised, painted poly frame with a divider running through the center from side to side. The poly frame was painted to match the exterior color of the cab. The Typhoon was offered with engines ranging from 330 horsepower to 370 horsepower. As with all of the previous new chassis introductions, the use of the Typhoon would expand beyond pumpers into the aerial market. At the same time it introduced the Typhoon chassis, E-ONE updated the Hush Series chassis to include the Cummins ISL engine. The first unit was delivered to Waukesha, Wisconsin.

During the summer of 2001, the Tradition Series was introduced. This was a value line of products for departments that were looking for less expensive alternatives to the fully customized apparatus. The HP75 aerials in this series would be offered on the Spartan Advantage/E-ONE super commercial chassis.

E-ONE unveiled two new additions to the aerial product line at the FRI trade show in New Orleans during August of 2001. The first was the F100 RLP, an addition to the line of Bronto Skylift aerials. The second new product was the HP95, a 95-foot, midship-mounted aerial platform.

The F100 RLP (Rescue Ladder Platform) was designed to combine the attributes of a Bronto with the truck requirements of the U.S. fire service. Items that needed to be addressed concerning the existing 91-foot, 118-foot, and 135-foot line of Bronto aerials included travel height, hose bed capacity, and ground-ladder storage. E-ONE needed a Bronto that would fit into a 12-foot fire station door. The current Bronto models had a travel height of 12 feet, 5 inches. The F100 RLP was released with a travel height of 11 feet, 9 inches. Additionally, the other Bronto units were designed for non-U.S. markets with different requirements. The Bronto torque box, for instance, would not allow for the interior storage of ground ladders common to other domestic aerials. Bronto ground ladders stored on aerials with bodies built by E-ONE required stacking the ladders horizontally above the low side compartments.

One of E-ONE's newest aerial units is the F100RLP, 100-foot Bronto Skylift, introduced in 2001. This was the first Bronto unit designed to offer features tailored specifically for the U.S. fire service, including the ability to carry a full complement of ground ladders and having enough compartment space to carry all of the equipment needed by fire departments. The articulated jib at the end of the telescoping boom provides tremendous flexibility for firefighters to overcome many different types of obstacles, including parapet walls, trees, and operations below grade.

This made it cumbersome to retrieve some of the ladders and minimized the space available for a full complement of ladders. The width of the torque box also hampered the amount of storage space on the outside of the body. The hose bed was only capable of holding 500 feet of 5-inch hose instead of the 1,000 feet that the rest of the industry was capable of accommodating. Lastly, the amount of compartment space for equipment was extremely limited and prevented some departments from carrying everything that they wanted.

Design of the F100 RLP began in the early part of 2000. E-ONE wanted the 11-feet, 9-inch clearance, and the ability to store 1,000 feet of 5-inch hose and to load this hose without lifting the aerial boom. The new unit had to have 120 cubic feet of compartment space and needed to accommodate a U.S. complement of standard ground ladders inside the torque box. The boom style also needed to be the HDT Series, and the length could reach anywhere from 100 feet or greater.

The result was a 100-foot HDT Series aerial that stored the jib along the main boom section instead of underneath it to achieve the lower travel height. The jib section had an offset in the boom to allow the bucket to duck underneath for storage below the boom, like the other HDT Series units. Saulsbury, a sister company of E-ONE and a member of the Fire Rescue Group of Federal Signal Corporation, built the body for the F100 RLP. It was fabricated out of stainless steel with 175 cubic feet of compartment storage space, well in excess of the minimum requirements set by E-ONE. The demo featured a 2,000 gallon-per-minute pump and a 300-gallon water tank. The tip load was rated at 1,000 pounds dry and 750 pounds while flowing 1,000 gallons per minute from the monitor nozzle at the bucket, in addition to allowing for 218 pounds of equipment mounted in the platform. The length of the jib boom was 22 feet.

The HP95 midship aerial platform was a four-section, diamond-extruded aerial with a 1,000-pound dry tip load

The F100RLP provides a conventional ladder alongside the solid boom design. Strength and stability are demonstrated here with nine firefighters along the length of the extended boom and in the platform. Computerized self-leveling of the unit simplifies deployment at a fire scene on level or uneven surfaces.

and a 500-pound wet rating, in addition to having the capacity for 305 pounds of equipment mounted in the bucket. Built on a Cyclone II chassis only, it had a jack spread of 15 feet, 6 inches for two scissors style jacks located under the turntable. The jacks were designed as stabilizers to provide tip-over stability. The HP95 utilized four leveling jacks that handled front-to-back and side-to-side leveling of the unit with an automatic leveling system prior to setting the outriggers. Two leveling jacks were placed behind the cab and the other two at the rear. These jacks went straight down. The HP95 was offered with a pump, a 300-gallon water tank, a side-stacker style body, and a travel height of 10 feet, 10 inches. When specified without a pump and water tank, the unit was designated an HP94 and had a travel height of 9 feet, 10 inches.

HME

In 2000, HME released the 1871 SL*e* Series cab and chassis for pumpers and aerials. This was the company's millennium cab and chassis, which was first displayed at the 2000 FRI in Dallas, Texas. The prototype for this totally new product featured a contoured front end with round headlights and turn signals that were recessed into the cab face. The grille had a distinct look with a crisscross diagonal pattern of twisted metal strands. The grille surround was formed of a poly material that was originally painted black, but later changed to match the color of the cab.

The SL*e*, where the "*e*" represents *e*-commerce and HME's commitment to the Internet, was designed and debuted on the Web before the public ever saw the prototype. Suggestions for refinements to the original design were solicited via the Internet.

This new product has a sophisticated electronic system that gives HME engineers and mechanics the opportunity to service or troubleshoot an SL*e* digitally via the telephone. The units have a standard phone jack that can allow HME to view the on-board electronic engine controls and other electrical components long distance. New engine control programs can be downloaded directly into the vehicle. The first SL*e* aerial was built as a demo unit with an R.K. Aerials 75-foot ladder and a body by Central States.

In 2002, HME changed its focus from being the largest independent supplier of custom fire truck chassis in the U.S. to becoming a supplier of a complete line of fire apparatus. HME has designed custom modular bodies that are fabricated from stainless steel. The body panels are precision cut by lasers and then bolted together. HME unveiled its first

complete rescue pumper at the FDIC in Indianapolis, Indiana. This unit, fabricated from stainless steel, featured an SFO cab and chassis. Also unveiled with the rescue pumper was a pumper/tanker on a commercial Navistar chassis, and a 75-foot aerial ladder by R.K. with an SL*e* chassis and a tanker on an 1871-P chassis. These and other products are part of the initial offerings through a new nationwide network of dealers.

HME wanted to revitalize a portion of fire service history with another addition to the new HME apparatus program. The company licensed the Ahrens Fox name, which will represent a complete line of new stainless steel HME bodies when they are mounted on one of the SL*e* chassis.

KME

In 2001, KME completely redesigned the 75-foot Fire Stix. KME changed the double acting extension cylinder to a single acting cylinder and went from one lift cylinder to dual lift cylinders, similar to the heavy-duty ladders. Mt. Pleasant, Pennsylvania, received the first redesigned Fire Stix in late 2001. Future plans called for performing similar changes to the 55-foot Fire Stix.

Many aerial ladders and platforms currently offer accessories as a means of increasing the unit's versatility for firefighters. Here, firefighters demonstrate the lifeline accessories attached to the tip of a Pierce aerial ladder to perform a rope rescue. Two firefighters on the ground tether the lines attached to the stokes basket, working in conjunction with the ladder operator to steady the retrieval of an injured person.

Also in 2001, KME introduced a five-section, 100-foot, mid-mount aerial ladder. This was the mid-mount platform without the bucket and was rated at 750 pounds dry and 500 pounds wet. The unit could have been rated much higher since the platform had a 1,000-pound rating and the aerial did not have to factor in the weight of the bucket. The jack spread of 18 feet and the use of four H-style outriggers was the same for both units. The first truck of this style was delivered to West Deptford Township, New Jersey, in May 2001.

Pierce

Two new aerials were introduced in 2000. The first was a mid-mount aerial platform. It had a 1,000-pound dry rating and a 500-pound wet rating. The five-section ladder had a length of 95 feet and used two midship, H-style outriggers with an 18-foot spread plus two rear outriggers with a 16-foot spread. Unlike some of the other midship aerial platforms on the market, the Pierce unit did not require downriggers or other front-end stabilization. Travel height was a low 9 feet, 10 inches. The first midship, 95-foot aerial platform built had job number 10970, but the first unit delivered to a customer went to Plymouth, Indiana, in April of 2001 with job number 12043. Pierce also built a 100-foot, midship, heavy-duty aerial ladder. This was a different unit from the midship aerial platform, not an aerial platform with the bucket removed. The ladder was also a five-section design. It utilized the same four outriggers and jack spread

This 2000 model year, 105-foot, Pierce aerial ladder was built on a Dash 2000 chassis with ALL-STEER capabilities for Aberdeen, Maryland. All of the axles are turned, demonstrating the excellent maneuverability for navigating through tight areas. Although the area where the truck is sitting has plenty of room on either side, the unit is shown being short jacked. This allows operations off one side of the truck with full outrigger deployment, even when the opposite side does not have sufficient room to extend the other outriggers. Ground-ladder storage is located within the center of the body, running through the torque box. This feature allows for the maximum amount of compartments on both sides of the vehicle.

The Pierce Sky-Arm is a versatile aerial that combines a four-section, 100-foot, tower ladder with an articulating fly section to increase the operating range. Clearwater, Florida, purchased this unit in 2000 on a Dash 2000 chassis without a pump or water tank. The articulating jib allows for below-grade operations, and also offers reach up and over stationary obstacles for a safer means of egress without having to use a separate, portable roof ladder.

as the aerial platform, and offered a 750-pound rating wet or dry. In July 2001, Ft. Wayne, Indiana, received the first 100-foot, midship ladder that was built. This unit had a 2,000 gallon-per-minute pump, 270 gallons of on-board water, and job number 10982. Madison Hose Co., Number 1, of Madison, Connecticut, was the first to put one of these 100-foot, midship ladders into service when the company received job number 10425 in November of 2000.

In 2002, Pierce had preliminary plans to add a TDA with a 750-pound tip load to the aerial family.

R.K. Aerials

In the year 2000, R.K. Aerials became part of the Rosenbauer America Group of companies, which included Rosenbauer International, Central States Fire Apparatus, Metz, and General Safety Equipment. This affiliation meant that Rosenbauer would have an aerial supplier for its apparatus companies, and at the same time meant that R.K. would not lose Central States and General to other ladder fabricators. Also in 2000, Quality Manufacturing and Luverne both requested that R.K. supply them with aerials.

Previously, these two companies sold units with ladders by Aerial Innovations. Thibault in Canada had also contracted with R.K. Aerials for the purchase of ladders and platforms.

At the 2001 FDIC in Indianapolis, Rosenbauer America introduced a line of custom fire truck chassis called the Commander. The 3000 Series, 4000 Series, and 5000 Series made up the line. Each model differed by the available horsepower ratings. The Commander 3000 featured 300–399 horsepower engines, the 4000 featured 400–499 horsepower, and the 5000 Series featured engines with 500 or more horsepower. This chassis allowed the Rosenbauer group of companies to offer a single-source product to those departments that requested it. In short, this meant that the chassis, body, and aerial were all built and supplied by the same company.

Some features of the new Commander were a fully contoured front that included recessed housings for all of the lights on the cab face and the emergency light bar at the roofline. The tilt-cab had a grill with horizontal slats in the center of the cab and barrier clearing short doors. Rosenbauer also boasted of increased interior space, improved visibility, lower cab floors, and improved placement of the air conditioner, auxiliary heaters, and a multiplexing electrical system that integrated the cab and body electrical systems into one cohesive unit. Six lengths were offered for the cab configurations based on an MFD design for seating of up to 10 firefighters.

In 2002 R.K. Aerials added Westates to the list of OEMs. In the works at the same time were product enhancements to

When Oshkosh Truck Corporation, Pierce's parent company, purchased Nova Quintech in 1998, one of the products that was sought after was the Sky-Boom telescoping water tower to compete with the Tele-Squrt from Snorkel. In 2001, Provo, Utah, purchased five Pierce units, two of which had Sky-Boom 55-foot, telescoping water towers. The entire Provo order was built on Quantum chassis and included a heavy rescue unit plus two 105-foot rear-mounted aerial ladders with ALL-STEER computerized steering.

The Fire Department in Yaphank on New York's Long Island purchased one of the first Pierce 95-foot, mid-mount, platform aerials in 2000. The unit is a full quint with a 2,000 gallon-per-minute pump and 300 gallons of water. The Pierce Dash 2000 chassis has become a best-selling aerial chassis for Pierce in recent years.

increase the tip load of the straight aerial ladders from 500 pounds to 750 pounds. As a means of filling a void created by the closure of Aerial Inovations, new products going through stages of design included a four-section, 100-foot, tractor-drawn aerial with a 500-pound tip load, and possibly a tiller quint to follow. Another new project in the works was a five-section, 100-foot, mid-mount aerial platform with a 1,000-pound dry rating and a 500-pound wet rating. Over 170 R.K. Aerials straight ladders and 15 aerial platforms are in service in the United States, Canada, Korea, and South America.

Schwing

In 2000, Schwing introduced the GLA high-flow FireArm water tower. This was a 90-foot articulated boom with a stainless steel 8-inch monitor and a 5,000 gallon-per-minute capacity. The truck apparatus body was also introduced in stainless steel.

In February of 2001, Schwing America and Pierce entered into an alliance whereby Pierce would have the exclusive rights to market the Schwing GLA Series articulated, high-volume booms. Pierce would offer the GLA 85 and GLA 90, three-section master stream devices capable of discharging up to 5,000 gallons of water or foam per minute. These units also had the ability to discharge the extinguishing agent from a distance up to 400 feet away from the fire. When assembled, these units would be marketed on the Pierce Dash 2000, Lance 2000, and Quantum chassis.

Seagrave

The Seagrave aerial line is made up of the Apollo aerial platform and the Patriot Series. The Apollo has a 105-foot reach with a 1,000-pound capacity in the platform and uses four H-style outriggers with a spread of 17 feet, 10 inches. The three-section ladder unit has a 2,000 gallon-per-minute waterway. The body is configured for center stack ground-ladder storage, and the Apollo is available as a straight truck or as a quint with a midship-mounted pump and a water tank. One monitor is standard at the platform with an option for a second.

The Patriot Series consists of the three-section, 75-foot, rear-mounted Mean Stick and the 100-foot rear-mount, or

the 100-foot TDA, both of which are four-section units. The Mean Stick has a 500-pound rating while flowing 1,000 gallons of water per minute in any position when fully extended. Hale or Waterous pumps can be specified with water tank sizes to 500 gallons. While the Mean Stick primarily utilizes a single-axle chassis with two rear H-style outriggers, it is available with a tandem axle using the same outriggers with Seagrave's standard-height fixed or tilt-cab. A pre-piped, pinnable waterway is standard for the Mean Stick. A low-profile cab option is also available for a 75-foot Patriot, but it does not meet the criteria for being a Mean Stick with the same compartment space.

The 100-foot rear-mount is available in two configurations. The base model has a 250-pound tip load. This has been one of the most popular trucks with large city departments such as FDNY and Chicago. As of 2001, the 500-pound-tip-rated Patriot rear-mount is called the Force. Like the Mean Stick, it maintains a 500-pound tip load rating while flowing 1,000 gallons of water per minute in any position. The Force can be ordered as a quint or without a pump and water tank. When using a standard-height custom cab, the Force requires a tandem-axle chassis with two rear-mounted H-style outriggers plus two A-style jacks mounted directly behind the cab. The A-style jacks do not extend past the width of the truck's body when deployed. This feature is unique to Seagrave and allows the operator more flexibility to spot the aerial in tight spaces. It is only necessary to ensure

This is a 75-foot 2000 Seagrave Mean Stick belonging to Radcliff, Kentucky. It features a short wheelbase, a truck complement of ground ladders, and has ladder controls at the turntable. This unit differs from the P-75, which places aerial controls at the pump panel and offers an engine's complement of ground ladders.

wider clearance for the rear of the vehicle instead of needing the added space for the forward stabilizers. When the Force is built with a low-profile Seagrave cab, however, it shares a torque box with the Apollo and uses all four H-style outriggers. A pre-piped waterway is available with a pinnable option on the Force.

The Patriot TDA has a 250-pound tip load. It is offered with a pre-piped, pinnable waterway, which requires the optional H-style outriggers with a 17-foot spread. Otherwise the TDA uses two compact A-style jacks. Either way, stabilizers on a TDA are located at the front section of the trailer body. Bodies are available in galvaneal or stainless steel. Center stack ground-ladder storage can be arranged with ladders placed horizontally or vertically.

The Seagrave custom chassis options for aerials include the all-steel J-Series fixed cabs and the T-Series tilt-cabs. The J-Series has seating for six firefighters and is offered in a conventional height or a low-profile version with a raised roof above each of the rear seating areas. Most aerials feature the popular T-Series tilt-cabs. Offered in full-tilt or split-tilt versions, Seagrave has a long four-door model with seating for six, an extended, long, four-door model with seating for up to eight, and an extra long four-door model that can accommodate up to ten people. The extra-long model is only available as a split tilt-cab. All of the T-Series cabs have available 10-inch or 15-inch raised roof options. Seating arrangements and cab storage compartments provide for a multitude of interior layouts.

In 2000 at the FRI trade show in Dallas, Seagrave introduced its newest cab and chassis pumper design called the Flame. This new lower cost product made the Seagrave product line available to fire departments that were unable to invest in a full, top-of-the-line custom pumper. A smaller Series 40 engine, simpler styling, a flat grill, barrier clearing short doors, seating for up to eight firefighters, and all-aluminum construction are some of the features of this new product. Although mention of a pumper in a book devoted to aerials may seem out of place, it is important to document this newest product offering due to the possibility that it will be adapted to accommodate aerial devices in the future.

Smeal

In 2000, Smeal added a new product to the line of rear-mounted aerial ladders—a 125-foot model. This steel aerial ladder has four sections, a 500-pound tip load while flowing 1,250 gallons of water per minute, and four H-style outriggers with an 18-foot spread for stabilization. The aerial is available on standard or low-profile chassis from HME or Spartan. The first delivery of the 125-foot model included two units for the St. Louis City Fire Department, as part of its fleet replacement program. The fleet consisted of thirty 75-foot Smeal quints and one 100-foot Smeal aerial platform, all of which were built on Spartan chassis.

The Smeal aerial product line currently consists of six heavy-duty aerial ladders and three aerial platforms. The aerial ladders are offered in 55-, 75-, 100-, 105-, and 125-foot lengths as rear-mounts, along with a 100-foot, five-section mid-mount. The rear-mounts are built with two, three, and four steel sections. The 55-foot model is named the Quintessential. All of the aerials have a 500-pound tip load while flowing 1,250 gallons per minute of water with the exception of the 100-foot model. Smeal calls this a super heavy-duty aerial with a 1,500-pound tip load while flowing 2,000 gallons per minute of water. Smeal offers a bolt-on egress ladder to the tip of the fly section. This simplifies replacement in the event of damage to the ladder tip. H-style outriggers are used to stabilize the aerials. Two rear outriggers are used for the 55-foot model, two rear outriggers plus two optional downriggers are placed behind the cab on the 75-foot model, and four outriggers are used for the 100-foot, 105-foot, and 125-foot ladders. The optional front downriggers on the 75-foot model increase the stability of the unit and eliminate the need for the front tires to be used to transfer part of the load during aerial operation.

The 55-foot quint can carry up to 500 gallons of water as well as a pumper complement of ground ladders, or it can be configured for a truck complement of ground ladders. The 75-foot quint on a single-axle chassis has a maximum water tank capacity of 400 gallons, while the tank size increases to 500 gallons with a tandem rear axle. The 105-foot quint carries a maximum of 400 gallons of water.

Smeal also offers a model UT100 rear-mount. This was designed to fit under a 10-foot door to accommodate older fire stations. This four-section, steel, medium-duty ladder has a smaller tip load of 500 pounds when dry or 250 pounds while flowing water.

The mid-mount aerial ladder has a 500-pound tip load while flowing 1,250 gallons of water per minute. Like all of the Smeal products, a Hale or Waterous pump can be specified and the aerials can accommodate up to 500 gallons of water.

Both the three-section, 85-foot and the four-section, 100-foot rear-mounted aerial platforms have the capacity to carry a maximum of 300 gallons of water. The platform itself offers 21 square feet of space with one standard monitor nozzle that can flow up to 1,500 gallons per minute, while dual monitors can flow 1,000 gallons per minute each, for a total output of 2,000 gallons of water. The tip load for both platforms is 500 pounds while flowing water and 1,000 pounds dry. Bodies are offered in aluminum as standard or galvaneal steel as an option. The units require tandem-axle chassis and utilize four H-style outriggers with the same specifications as the 105-foot aerial ladder.

Sutphen

Sutphen introduced a new five-section, 110-foot tower at the 2001 FRI convention in New Orleans. This unit featured a shorter overall length than the 100-foot model, due largely to increased overlap of each ladder section. Though similar, the box design of the ladder was slightly larger than on previous aerials and this new unit had some inherent changes in the turntable base. The platform was rated to carry 1,000 pounds and flow 2,000 gallons of water per minute. Stability was achieved with eight stabilizers, four on either side of the truck, only six of which are visible. There are two sets of outriggers, one set of rear down-riggers, and one set between the front axle and the frame to take weight off of the springs. Like all Sutphen aerial units since the mid-1990s, the body is fabricated from stainless steel and accommodates a 400-gallon water tank. The first production unit for the 110-foot Sutphen tower was built for the Green Township Fire Department in Cincinnati.

Index

About the author:

Larry Shapiro is a photographer whose experience spans more than 25 years. His portfolio includes work for private, corporate, and commercial clients, but his passion lays in his all consuming love of the fire service and all things motorized. During his career, he has provided photographic services for multiple fire truck manufacturers including Emergency One, Duplex, FMC, Grumman, Hendrickson, HME, Pemfab, Pierce, Seagrave, Snorkel, Spartan, and Sutphen, plus truck builders Freightliner, Oshkosh, Sterling, and Western Star, in the form of advertisements, calendars, and sales literature.

An author as well, he has written and provided the photography for multiple books including *Cranes in Action*, *Fighting Fire Trucks*, *Pumpers: Workhorse Fire Engines*, *Special Police Vehicles*, and *Tow Trucks in Action*. His current book, *Aerial Fire Trucks* adds to his collection of MBI Publishing Company titles, soon to be followed by another fire service book entitled *Hook & Ladders*.

Larry resides in a Chicago suburb with his wife and three sons.

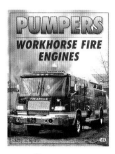
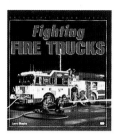
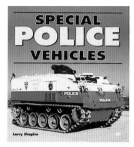
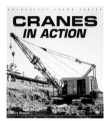
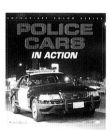

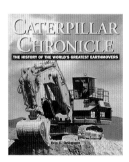
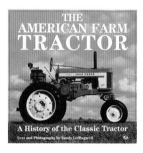